Practical Evaluation Guide

About the Series

The American Association for State and Local History Book Series addresses issues critical to the field of state and local history through interpretive, intellectual, scholarly, and educational texts. To submit a proposal or manuscript to the series, please request proposal guidelines from AASLH headquarters: AASLH Editorial Board, 1717 Church St., Nashville, Tennessee 37203. Telephone: (615) 320-3203. Website: www.aaslh.org.

About the Organization

The American Association for State and Local History (AASLH) is a national history membership association headquartered in Nashville, Tennessee. AASLH provides leadership and support for its members who preserve and interpret state and local history in order to make the past more meaningful to all Americans. AASLH members are leaders in preserving, researching, and interpreting traces of the American past to connect the people, thoughts, and events of yesterday with the creative memories and abiding concerns of people, communities, and our nation today. In addition to sponsorship of this book series, AASLH publishes *History News* magazine, a newsletter, technical leaflets and reports, and other materials; confers prizes and awards in recognition of outstanding achievement in the field; supports a broad education program and other activities designed to help members work more effectively; and advocates on behalf of the discipline of history. To join AASLH, go to www.aaslh.org or contact Membership Services, AASLH, 1717 Church St., Nashville, TN 37203.

Practical Evaluation Guide

Tools for Museums and Other Informal Educational Settings

Third Edition

Judy Diamond, Michael Horn,
and David H. Uttal

ROWMAN & LITTLEFIELD
Lanham • Boulder • New York • London

Published by Rowman & Littlefield
A wholly owned subsidiary of The Rowman & Littlefield Publishing Group, Inc.
4501 Forbes Boulevard, Suite 200, Lanham, Maryland 20706
www.rowman.com

Unit A, Whitacre Mews, 26-34 Stannary Street, London SE11 4AB

British Library Cataloguing in Publication Data

Library of Congress Cataloging-in-Publication Data Available

Names: Diamond, Judy, author. | Horn, Michael (Michael Stephen) author. |
    Uttal, David H. (David Henry), 1960– author.
Title: Practical evaluation guide : tools for museums and other informal educational
    settings / Judy Diamond, Michael Horn, and David H. Uttal.
Description: Third edition. | Lanham : Rowman & Littlefield, 2016. |
    Series: American Association for State and Local History | Includes bibliographical
    references and index.
Identifiers: LCCN 2015042901 (print) | LCCN 2015046192 (ebook) |
    ISBN 9781442263536 (cloth : alk. paper) | ISBN 9781442263543 (pbk. : alk. paper) |
    ISBN 9781442263550 (Electronic)
Subjects: LCSH: Museum exhibits—Evaluation. | Museums—Educational aspects. |
    Non-formal education.
Classification: LCC AM151 .D5 2016 (print) | LCC AM151 (ebook) |
    DDC 069/.5—dc23 LC record available at http://lccn.loc.gov/2015042901

Printed in the United States of America

Contents

List of Figures

List of Tables

Preface

A lot has happened in the world of informal science learning since the *Practical Evaluation Guide* was first published in 1999. The intervening years have seen the rise of mobile technologies, the emergence of social media, the widespread availability of streaming digital video, and the founding of Wikipedia. In many ways, the availability of accessible scientific information has never been greater. Yet, despite these changes and the economic turmoil of the past decade, informal learning institutions of all stripes have continued to thrive. The public still seeks out the enlightenment, exhilaration, and entertainment of museums, science centers, zoos, aquaria, planetariums, and nature centers. The need for high-quality evaluation of innovative programs and exhibits remains as strong as ever.

As its name implies, this volume is meant to serve as a handbook for students, evaluators, researchers, and other professionals interested in informal learning institutions and the audiences they serve. In this third edition, we strive to remain accessible and practical, while broadening our scope to embrace new technologies and developments in the practice of evaluation in informal science institutions. We thought the field of informal learning might embrace a more prescriptive approach to evaluation, following publication of the NSF-sponsored framework for evaluating the impacts of informal science education projects (Friedman 2008). In fact, the field has, if anything, become more eclectic. As researchers from a broad range of disciplines have turned their attention to informal science institutions, more creative techniques have been used to assess impacts with an even wider range of acceptable standards of excellence.

This book is divided into four parts. Part I addresses the design and conduct of studies of visitor learning, while Part II takes a more in-depth look at common evaluation tools, including interviews, observations, surveys, and questionnaires. Part III discusses the growing role of interactive digital media and new technologies for evaluation. Part IV discusses how to present and share results of evaluation studies with various stakeholders.

Each of us comes from different disciplines to participate in informal evaluation. Diamond's first evaluation studies were conducted of family groups at the Exploratorium in San Francisco, California, using the methods of ethology she utilized in studies of coyote social behavior (Diamond 1986). For her, the museum was an ideal setting to observe how human families engage in natural teaching and learning behaviors in a free-choice environment, giving insight into fundamental ways that human social groups interact with and learn from their environment. Just as in any field research, she had to maintain an open mind about what was observed, to use a light touch so participants would not be adversely influenced by the observer's presence, to employ rigorous methods for data collection, and to retain constraint and humility when interpreting results. Since that time, she has continued to research the behavior of animals in the wild, including a 20-year field study of parrots in New Zealand (Diamond & Bond 1999).

Michael Horn and David Uttal bring new expertise from their disciplines of psychology and computer science. These two individuals are shaping the future of multidisciplinary learning sciences, approaches that include studying how learning takes place in institutions and settings guided by free-choice and voluntary participation. Both are members of the Learning Sciences faculty in the School of Education and Social Policy at Northwestern University with joint appointments in Psychology (Uttal) and Computer Science (Horn).

David Uttal's research interests are in the development of symbolic and spatial thinking, which he studies in a variety of contexts: laboratories, classrooms, and informal learning environments. With Catherine Haden, he is studying how children and their parents communicate in children's museum, and how this communication continues outside the museum. Uttal's work on the development of spatial cognition has focused on how spatial thinking influences STEM learning and achievement. His meta-analysis of the malleability of spatial thinking, and the influences of training and experience, won the 2015 George Miller Award for Outstanding Contribution to General Psychology from Division 1 of the American Psychological Association.

Mike Horn has contributed a significant new section to this book that focuses on the opportunities and pitfalls of evaluating with digital media in informal settings. Horn thinks critically about the role of technology in museums and other informal learning spaces. Most of his work could be called "design-based research." That is, the only way to really understand appropriate uses of new technology is to build working prototypes, put them out in the real world, and carefully observe how people interact. This leads to numerous cycles of reflection and revision as a way to come up with broader insights.

Horn got his start by collaborating with the Museum of Science, Boston, Massachusetts, to create a computer programming and robotics exhibit. Visitors could use interlocking wooden tiles to build working computer programs that would control the movements of a robotic vacuum cleaner. Since then, he has designed and studied technology-based exhibits with institutions such as the California Academy of Sciences, the Field Museum, and the Computer History Museum.

Judy Diamond
Mike Horn
David Uttal

Acknowledgments

Many people helped to make this book possible through their support, encouragement, and expertise. Foremost, we thank Amy Spiegel, at the Center for Instructional Innovation at the University of Nebraska; Chia Shen and Florian Block, at the Harvard School of Computer Science and Engineering; Benjamin Jee, at the Department of Psychology of Worcester State University; Camillia Matuk, at the NYU Steinhardt School of Culture, Education, and Human Development; Margaret Evans, at University of Michigan Center for Human Growth and Development; Medha Tare, at the University of Maryland Center for Advanced Study of Language; Sherman Rosenfeld, from the Davidson Institute of Science Education at the Weizmann Institute of Science; Julia McQuillan, at the University of Nebraska Department of Sociology; Monique Scott, at the American Museum of Natural History; Rob Semper, at the Exploratorium; and Alan Bond, professor emeritus of Biological Sciences at the University of Nebraska. Finally, we thank Charles Harmon, our editor at the Rowman & Littlefield Publishing Group.

This book included work funded by grants from the National Science Foundation (grant no. 0229294, PI J. Diamond) and Science Educational Partnership (SEPA) awards from the National Institutes of Health (grants no. 1R25OD010506, PIs J. Diamond, J. McQuillan, C. Wood and R25RR024267, PIs J. Diamond, M. Rankin, C. Wood). The content described here is solely the responsibility of the authors and does not necessarily represent the official views of the NSF or NIH.

Part I

EVALUATING INFORMAL LEARNING

Evaluation is as much a mind-set as it is a set of methodologies. On paper, the planning and design of an evaluation study can appear to be linear and systematic, moving from articulating the study purpose to establishing evaluation objectives or questions to choosing methods. In reality, the process is much more iterative in nature. The evaluator cycles between tasks to create a study that will address the needs and expectations of various stakeholders and fit within constraints such as time and money. As Patton (1990, 2008) and others have noted, there is no one fixed recipe or algorithm for designing an evaluation study.

Evaluation planning sometimes starts by identifying a preferred method; for example, "I want focus groups conducted with museum members . . . or a phone survey in our community to determine why some people don't come to the zoo." Evaluators may need to put off talking about methods and instead encourage clients to articulate larger problems, questions, and institutional values. Sometimes, clients have a clear sense about what they need or what questions they want answered. Other times, evaluators need to work with clients to help draw out the issues at hand. A well-designed evaluation study is like peeling the bark off a tree trunk: Questions that frame the overall study then reveal inner layers that describe the overall design or approach, which, in turn, shape the methods that will provide data needed to answer those questions. Articulating the initial questions or need for the study is the fabric that weaves together the entire evaluation process.

Is there such a thing as a "good" evaluation question? There is no clear formula, but based on our experience, we recommend asking questions that identify areas important for an institution's goals or values and that translate into usable data for those interested in the study. When framing evaluation

1

questions, keep an open mind to the possibility of finding unanticipated information from the study.

In this section, we help you to get started with the planning of an evaluation study. Chapter 1 provides guidelines for evaluation design. Chapter 2 discusses learning outcomes you might consider when evaluating informal places or projects. Chapter 3 presents strategies that can be used to assess learning in informal environments, including measures of knowledge retention, conceptual change, implicit memory, and visual-spatial memory. Chapter 4 highlights how you can protect the rights and privacy of the participants who agree to be a part of your study.

Chapter 1

Thinking through an Evaluation Study

You want to study people at a museum, zoo, botanical garden, or any other informal educational place, but where do you begin? Do you want to know how an exhibit or program engages visitors? Or what it communicates to them? What improvements will make a real difference? Who uses the exhibit or participates in the program? And who is targeted, but does not participate? How do visitors share their experiences? And as a result, do they think about things differently? Overall, what are the different kinds of impacts of a particular program? Evaluations can help answer these questions, but there is no single recipe; each study should be designed to meet the specific needs of the institution, exhibit, or program being studied.

There are many kinds of evaluation studies, but most can be identified as one of the three types: front-end evaluation, formative evaluation, or summative evaluation. *Front-end evaluation* provides background information for future program planning (Dierking & Pollock 1998). It can reveal visitors' prior knowledge, experience, and expectations. Front-end evaluation can utilize surveys, interviews, or observations of typical behavior patterns, but it can also include historical data, archival materials, such as photographs, and comparisons to similar institutions or programs. A goal of front-end evaluation is to learn about the audience before a program or exhibit has been designed to better understand how visitors will eventually respond once the project has been developed. Essentially, front-end evaluation identifies information about visitors that can be incorporated into the project or program design.

Formative evaluation provides information about how well a program or exhibit works, how well it communicates to its intended audiences, and what changes would lead to better outcomes (Flagg 1990; Griggs & Manning

1983; Taylor 1991). Formative evaluation generally occurs while a project is under development, where the evaluator measures visitor responses to models, plans, or prototypes of the program or exhibit. A *prototype* is a working version of an interactive exhibit, label, or other component that closely resembles the functionality of the final product, although it may be more roughly constructed (Oppenheimer 1986). The more developed the model or prototype is, the more likely visitors in the formative stage will anticipate their reactions to the final product. Information from formative evaluation is used to make changes to improve the design of a program or exhibit before it is implemented. Additional formative evaluation can also occur once a program or exhibit opens. It is useful for troubleshooting problems, it informs museum staff and designers about simple improvements that can be made to maximize visitor experience, and it may address problems that could not be foreseen during the development of a program or exhibit, such as lighting, crowd flow, or signage issues (Diamond 1991). In fact, some institutions commit to a continuous iterative process of feedback and improvement throughout the life of an exhibit or program, so that formative evaluation is an ongoing activity (Semper 1990).

Summative evaluation attempts to understand the impact of a project after it is completed. It is conducted after the exhibit has been opened to the public and iterative design is complete, or after a program has been presented. Summative evaluation can be as simple as documenting who visits an exhibition or participates in a program, or it can be as complex as understanding how an exhibit experience changes the way in which visitors reason about a topic. Generally, the results of summative evaluation will be used to improve future activities through an understanding of existing programs (Kubota & Olstad 1991; McLean 1993; Paris 2002).

DEVELOPING AN EVALUATION PLAN

The first step in developing an evaluation plan is to decide the topic and scope of the study. The following questions serve as a guide:

- What is the purpose of the study? How will the results be used? Will your study provide information for planning (front end), for ongoing development and improvement (formative), or on the impacts of a project (summative)?
- Who is it for? Is your study being conducted for an internal or an external audience? Is it for decision makers, program staff, outside funders, other researchers, or for everyone? To whom will you present your report? Key people to consider may be internal to the institution, people like

administrators, educators, designers, curators, and members of the board of trustees, or they may be external, like community members, partners, consultants, and funders.

- Who will undertake the study? Will you use an internal evaluator (i.e., a staff member of the institution being studied), an external evaluator (i.e., an unaffiliated, evaluation professional), or faculty and/or students from a local university, social science research, or education departments?
- What is the budget for your study? Costs create boundaries for the scope of the study. These boundaries should be clarified and the implications should be discussed at the outset of the study.
- How do you hope to share the results of your study? Will you want a formal, written report? Will the findings be presented orally or through digital or social media? Do you plan to publish the results in journals, conferences, or trade publications?

After clarifying these questions, the next step is to prepare a written plan that will give interested parties a summary of what you intend to do. The plan should be readable and concise, and it should not overstate the scope of the study. Such a document gives interested parties the opportunity to learn about the study plan and provide necessary feedback. The following outline template serves as a guide for developing a written evaluation plan:

- *Project description*: In a page or two, describe the institution, program, or exhibit that you will be evaluating by including simple drawings or photographs, if appropriate. State the overall purpose and timeline of the evaluation study.
- *Evaluation objectives*: What are the key questions or issues that will frame your evaluation study? For example, you might want to know about visitors' interests, attitudes, or perceptions toward a potential exhibit topic, or you may be interested in knowing the extent to which a school program enhances students' critical thinking skills. So that expectations are clear, it is sometimes useful to mention those things that you do *not* plan to evaluate within the program, exhibit, or institution.
- *Evaluation design*: Outline the design or the overall approach of your study in a couple of paragraphs. For example, is your study experimental or quasi-experimental, designed to investigate the effect of a particular treatment on visitors? Or is it descriptive, intended to better understand a particular phenomenon or audience? Will your study have a longitudinal component in which you collect data from people at more than one point in time?
- *Methods*: Indicate which methods you plan to use to collect your data. For example, you might say that you will conduct observations and interviews

of a sample of 50 typical museum visitors while they are using an exhibit prototype. Or you may state that you will conduct phone interviews with 150 program participants. Wherever possible, consider using multiple methods that will permit a more detailed understanding of your question or issue from various perspectives. Specify whether you plan to use both qualitative findings, which summarize subjects' responses and interpretations in narrative form, and quantitative data, which uses statistical analysis to summarize the results.

- *Proposed timeline*: State when the evaluation study will begin, when data will be collected, and when the final report will be completed. Be realistic in your time commitments. Consider daily, weekly, or seasonal variations in visitor use when you estimate how long it will take to collect the data.
- *Products*: A brief summary report, followed by a more lengthy background report, can be very useful. Many people will be primarily interested in the summary, but sometimes, it is also helpful to provide a debriefing session for the groups most interested in your study.

As you write your evaluation plan, keep in mind that your audience may be broader than you expect. Try to use everyday language and explain terminology. For example, *quasi-experimental* may not be a term that everyone is familiar with.

Evaluators sometimes use logic models as tools for planning and evaluating informal learning projects. A *logic model* is a visual depiction, often in matrix form, of the linkages between a project's goals, activities, and expected outcomes (see additional examples in W. K. Kellogg Foundation 2004; National Science Foundation 2010). For project staff, logic models help to clarify the purpose of a project and facilitate communication of that purpose. A logic model can serve as a road map for staff, helping them to know where they are going, and how they will know when they get there. For evaluators, logic models ensure that project outcomes are clearly articulated at the outset and are well aligned with project activities (see Figure 1.1). Some funding agencies are now asking for logic models to be included in grant proposals, and many evaluators are incorporating the development of logic models into the planning and design of their studies.

After having developed your evaluation plan, share it with interested parties and engage them in discussion of the key objectives, design, and proposed methods, encouraging them to provide critical feedback. An evaluation plan is not a fixed entity; it is a working document that evolves as staff and community members respond and offer their perspectives and insights on the study.

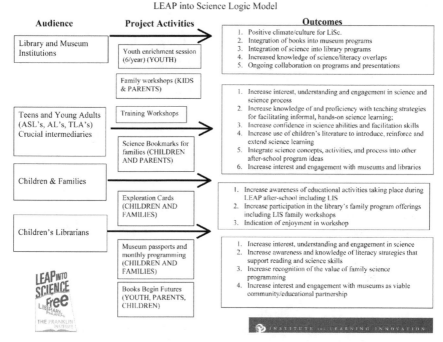

Figure 1.1 **A logic model developed by the Institute for Learning Innovation for The Franklin Institute Science Museum's LEAP into Science project.** *Source*: Courtesy of The Franklin Institute and the Institute for Learning Innovation.

EVALUATION IN CONTEXT

Evaluation occurs within social, cultural, historical, and political contexts— both for the institution conducting the evaluation and for the visitors or communities that will participate in the study. With that in mind, evaluators need to be fully aware of the context into which they are entering, including its complexities and nuances:

> One hallmark of evaluative responsiveness . . . is the evaluator's recognition, appreciation, and incorporation of culturally related contextual factors into his or her practice. The contextual factors include many of the more readily discussed dimensions of culture, including the demographics and some aspects of socioeconomic factors. But these factors also include the less spoken issues of power, institutional racism, and social justice. [SenGupta, Hopson, & Thompson-Robinson 2004, p. 11]

Evaluators have identified numerous strategies for conducting culturally responsive evaluation (Jolly 2002; National Science Foundation 2000, 2002).

Culture here refers not only to ethnic or racial background but also to components of identity such as age, gender, sexual orientation, socioeconomic status, and any other factors that may be relevant within a specific context. The following strategies will help you design an evaluation study that is sensitive and appropriate for a diverse range of audiences:

- Be sensitive to the needs and rights of evaluation participants, ensuring that your study does not detract from their overall museum experience and that visitors have the option of not participating if they so choose.
- Ensure that the evaluation questions are appropriately framed. In a culturally responsive study, the questions will have to be carefully considered not only by the evaluator and project staff but also by others who are part of or closely connected to the target audience(s) of the study.
- Do *not* make assumptions about the culture you are working in. According to Frierson, Hood, and Hughes (2002), sensitivity to your audience's beliefs, values, and ways of viewing the world will increase the likelihood that your study is truly responsive and relevant to that particular context. Keep in mind that all those involved in conducting the evaluation (from designing the study to collecting and interpreting data) also bring a particular "worldview," or a way of seeing and interpreting the world, which may be different from that of the community you are working with.
- Be aware of institutional values. Museums have implicit cultures, each with particular values and ways of working. In evaluating programs and exhibits in museums, it is important to pay careful attention to the language used and the processes engaged in. This language will often imply a set of values about the relationship between institutions and the communities they serve.
- Do *not* assume that all members of a cultural group think, feel, and see the world in the same way. Although there is naturally some overlap that links a group together, each individual has a different connection or will likely have a different experience of a museum program or exhibition. Elders of a cultural group may respond very differently than do their children or grandchildren. Gender, sexual orientation, age, religion, and life experiences all lead to individual diversity in responses. Thus, it is essential in evaluation that you seek and encourage multiple views.
- Consider finding cultural guides, people who operate easily in two or more cultures, to guide you to gain access, trust, and respect within the culture or community you are interested in. Such guides can help you communicate in the preferred language of your subjects as well as the specific cultural protocols that one must be familiar with when working with many communities. Your guides can provide deeper understanding of and relationship to the culture than an outsider can gain in a short amount of time. Such guides

can also help you understand a community's history, experience, and attitudes toward evaluation, which may influence how people respond to your study.

- Consider a participatory or collaborative approach to evaluation. This requires engaging a community on a deep level, in which community members contribute to developing important evaluation questions, best methods for answering those questions within the cultural context, and ways of interpreting the data.

Chapter 2

Informal Learning

Many evaluation studies will touch on how people learn in informal environments. In the last two decades, progress has been made in our understanding of how museums, zoos, aquaria, and nature centers affect people's lives, resulting in an increased appreciation for the complexity of learning as it happens outside of school walls. This chapter considers ways of addressing informal learning and highlights some of the key characteristics and outcomes relevant for evaluators working in informal environments.

DEFINING INFORMAL LEARNING

Various terms have been used to describe the learning that takes place in museums, zoos, botanic gardens, aquaria, and nature centers. It is referred to as informal learning, out-of-school learning, broader impacts, non-formal learning, and free-choice learning (Falk 2001). Terminology aside, what is common across all of these terms is an emphasis on the learning that occurs outside of the formal education system, in which the learner has choice and control over his or her experience. Broadly speaking, informal learning has the following characteristics (National Research Council 2009):

- It is voluntary (no one is mandated to learn).
- It is learner-motivated, self-directed, guided by intrinsic interests, curiosity, and exploration.
- It is nonlinear and open-ended.
- Unlike schools, with grades and tests, informal learning has no performance measures.

- It can occur in a variety of settings, including institutions such as museums, zoos, botanical gardens, nature centers, and aquaria; programs such as camps, fairs, festivals, and clubs; and locations such as playgrounds, parks, and even street corners.
- It is both ubiquitous and ongoing—it occurs in many places, at any time of the day, and at any time of one's life. It can be instantaneous or last an entire lifetime.
- It is often mediated within a social context. People learn informally with friends, family, and even strangers (see Figure 2.1).

Frank Oppenheimer, founding director of the Exploratorium in San Francisco, California, pointed out that informal learning generally does not confer levels of accomplishment or degrees; there are no prerequisites, you cannot graduate from informal learning, and you cannot fail:

> Museums are a vast resource of props for discovery; they can relieve any of the tensions which make learning in school ineffective or even painful. No one ever "fails" in a museum. One museum is not a prerequisite for the next. [Oppenheimer & Cole 1974, p. 8]

Figure 2.1 Social interactions are part of how visitors explore the Tree of Life exhibits at the California Academy of Sciences in San Francisco. *Source*: A. D. McCormick ©2015 California Academy of Sciences. see https://lifeonearth.seas.harvard.edu).

The distinctions between informal and formal learning may sometimes blur. Classes are taught in museums and zoos, and sometimes these are mandated or structured; they follow a curriculum, and result in grades. Increasingly, there are efforts to interweave the programs of informal learning institutions with those of schools (Hofstein & Rosenfeld 1996). Several museums operate public accredited schools where students participate in both school and museum activities. There are thus many different gradations that combine elements of museum and school or of zoo and school. For example, the Lincoln Children's Zoo in Nebraska cooperates with the public high school district to offer a four-year science focus program as an alternative to conventional high school. The museums in Balboa Park in San Diego, California, cooperate in "School in the Park" where inner city school classrooms spend between one and two months in week-long programs at ten informal institutions. Bridging the gap between formal and informal education can increase student motivation for learning, expand student conceptions of learning and knowledge, and help students develop new skills and abilities (Fallik, Rosenfeld, & Eylon 2013; Semper 1990). Informal education can create flexibility in teacher-student relationship, moving from hierarchical relationships to that of mutual guidance.

Informal learning prepares people for lifelong learning. People experience learning as part of everyday life, and they believe that it requires initiative, and that everyone, regardless of background, is allowed to participate. Informal learning reinforces learning for its own sake, and reminds us that learning can be both fun and exciting.

CHARACTERISTICS OF INFORMAL LEARNING

Informal learning is personal and individualized. People choose whether or not to visit informal institutions and, when they are there, decide how they will engage with exhibits, programs, and activities. Each visitor has a unique, personal experience shaped by a range of emotional, social, cultural, and biological factors. Evaluation, therefore, takes into account the individual's agenda and the ways in which visitors construct their own meaning and understanding during their museum experience.

Informal learning is frequently an intensely social experience occurring in the company of family or friends. Adults and children, for example, often have a social dynamic that leads to more time at exhibits and more in-depth experiences (Diamond, Smith, & Bond 1988; Zimmerman, Reeve, & Bell 2010). Informal learning also offers opportunities for people to learn from the behavior of others. In museums, the experience of observing others at an interactive exhibit can be just as compelling as directly manipulating it

(Diamond 1986; Tare et al. 2011). Informal learning also involves teaching, where group members direct and reinforce each other's attention and actions. Diamond (1980) and Dierking (1987) showed that among families visiting museums, teaching is likely to be reciprocal, with children likely to teach adults and vice versa. Researchers have shown the important role that conversations play in learning in the museum, because group members share thoughts and ideas, ask each other questions, and work together to make meaning out of experiences (Allen 2002; Leinhardt, Crowley, & Knutson 2002; Tare et al. 2011).

An important aspect of the social context involves play, which can be either solitary or social. In museums, zoos, and parks, play is not only tolerated but also encouraged. People who play at exhibits often spend more time with them and manipulate them in unexpected ways, which can lead to a more thorough knowledge of exhibit phenomena (Diamond 1996; Lucas & McManus 1986). Play can also be part of the informal teaching process. At the Exploratorium, the teenage Explainers use play not only as a means of entertainment but also as a way of demonstrating exhibit operations to the public (Diamond et al. 1987; see also Singer & Golinkoff 2006).

Oppenheimer pointed out many years ago that play and exploration become the means for experiencing the informal environment in a personal and individualized way:

> A large part of the play of children involves using common physical and cultural components of society in a context that is divorced from its primary purpose. It is through such inventive and repetitive play that they learn to feel at home with the world. In this fashion our exhibits are also playful. . . . In exhibits that are obviously intended for play, exhibits that themselves use props divorced from their original context, all manner of lovely things are discoverable, even by the people who invent them. [Oppenheimer 1972, p. 982]

Informal learning occurs over time and across space. Informal learning involves making links to, or between, previously separate ideas (Falk 2004). It is cumulative and iterative, an ongoing, lifelong process rather than a single event. Many researchers and evaluators have advocated a wider time frame for assessment to understand how visitors integrate museum visits into the rest of their lives.

Researchers have examined how a learner's prior knowledge and convictions shape the way in which she or he develops new understandings. A learner's prior knowledge can confound the best efforts to deliver ideas accurately (see Davis, Horn, & Sherin 2013). There is widespread agreement that prior knowledge influences learning and that learners construct concepts from prior knowledge. Learning proceeds primarily from prior knowledge and only secondarily from the exhibit or program. Prior knowledge greatly affects what we learn from experience; it can both interfere with and facilitate learning. Jeremy Roschelle (1995) calls this the "paradox of continuity." He suggests a few guidelines for designers of interactive experiences:

> First, designers should seek to refine prior knowledge, not attempt to replace learners' understanding with their own. Second, designers must anticipate a long-term learning process, of which the short-term experience will form an incremental part. Third, designers must remember that learning depends on social interaction; conversations shape the form and content of the concepts that learners construct. Only part of specialized knowledge can exist explicitly as information; the rest must come from engagement in the practice of discourse of the community. [Roschelle 1995:40]

INFORMAL LEARNING OUTCOMES

Visits to informal learning environments rarely result in one kind of outcome. Museums, zoos, botanical gardens, aquaria, and nature centers are important forums for fostering learning that is salient in an individual's daily life (National Research Council 2009). Evaluating the outcomes of informal learning therefore is rarely as simple as giving visitors a test to see how much they learned.

The National Research Council (2009) and Friedman (2008) provide a useful framework for identifying the following informal learning outcomes:

- *Awareness or knowledge:* Much of what people learn in and from informal institutions relates to the awareness, knowledge, or understanding of particular phenomena. Informal learning experiences can result in the acquisition of implicit knowledge, and they can result in conceptual change.
- *Engagement or interest*: Informal learning settings can help people to become engaged or interested in a topic or activity. These in turn can generate excitement and motivation to learn. According to the National Research Council (2009), the emotions associated with interest are a major factor in thinking and learning, helping people learn as well as helping with what is retained and how long it is remembered. In other words, the degree to which we are interested in something influences how we learn about it, and informal institutions are particularly good places for generating personal interest.
- *Attitudes:* Learning from informal environments can result in changes in long-term perspectives toward particular phenomena, topics, or activities. For example, studies investigating the impact of museum youth programs

found that sustained participation in these programs can increase not only youths' self-confidence and self-esteem but also their attitudes toward academic and career possibilities in the future (Diamond et al. 1987; Luke et al. 2007).

- *Behavior and skills:* Informal learning experiences can result in changed behavior and thinking skills on the part of visitors. Informal learning environments can provide opportunities for people to engage in inquiry—to ask questions, explore ideas, experiment, apply their ideas, make predictions, draw conclusions, and provide evidence to support their thinking. In a study investigating the impacts of a multiple-visit program for elementary students, researchers found that participating students demonstrated more advanced critical thinking skills, including but not limited to the ability to provide evidence in support of an interpretation of a work of art (Adams, Foutz, Luke, & Stein 2005).

In addition to the outcomes identified, the National Research Council (2009) emphasizes that museums can stimulate and support the formation of learning identities (see also Falk 2006). For instance, visitors can come to see themselves as science learners, as someone who knows about, uses, and sometimes contributes to science. People also reflect on their own learning processes and needs and view themselves as learners.

Evaluators working in informal settings need to remember that people generally choose to visit these environments, often with others in a heterogeneous group, and make use of them in ways that make the experience both individual and contextual in nature. Expected outcomes can include acquisition of implicit knowledge, generating interest and excitement in a topic or activity, and supporting visitors' reflections on who they are as learners.

Chapter 3

Measuring Learning

Informal educational experiences are diverse and generally unpredictable. Visitors spend their time observing, reading, playing, interacting socially, sometimes attending to personal needs, and often interacting with their surroundings. They observe exhibits, the actions of other visitors, demonstrations by staff, and other kinds of presentations. They interact with the environment by manipulating exhibits, moving through spaces, playing games, and socializing with other people. They spend time on smartphones and other devices, taking pictures, checking social media, and communicating with friends and family who may or may not be at the museum. They sometimes spend time reading—instructions, labels, signs, or brochures, and even books they bring along with them.

The complexity and diversity of learning in informal environments require that evaluators think carefully about the design and use of appropriate measures of learning. No single measure is ideal for all circumstances. Research design often involves trade-offs. For example, one may have to compromise on finding an ideal comparison group to make the research more relevant to museum learning. The goal of this chapter is to provide you with a toolkit of different research techniques to measure learning and to help you decide which techniques to use to answer different questions.

Why do we need rigorous study methods for measuring learning? Can't we just ask visitors what they have learned? For example, we could give visitors a survey as they leave the museum, asking them to rate how much they learned from their visit. Researchers refer to these sorts of assessment as *self-report measures,* because the visitor is reporting his or her own evaluation of learning. Although self-report measures can be helpful, they should rarely be relied on as the sole measure of learning. The reason is that people are often not accurate about assessing how much they have learned (Bjork and Linn

2006). For example, when people enjoy a museum visit, they may often think they have learned a great deal, even if that is not really the case. Therefore, avoid relying exclusively on self-report measures to understand what or how much visitors have learned.

MEASURING KNOWLEDGE RETENTION

One relatively simple form of learning involves the retention of information. For example, we might want to determine whether visitors learn the names of dinosaurs or the planets in our solar system. If assessing this kind of factual learning is our goal, then we can use measures of *recall* and *recognition*. *Recall* is the memory capacity used in quiz shows: The contestant is given a bare minimum of information to cue the answer, and she or he must search for the correct word or concept that fits the data supplied. You can think of recall as the memory required to answer a fill-in-the-blank item on a test. In contrast, *recognition* plays a role in cued retrieval of information, such as required in multiple-choice tests. In other words, you only have to recognize the correct answer from a list of choices. This is why modern computer systems use menu bars. It is a lot easier to remember what you want to do when you are presented with a short list of options to choose from.

In informal learning environments, where visitors are exposed to an enormous amount of different kinds of information, it is relatively difficult to test for recall. Visitors typically wander through a museum making their own decisions about what to pay attention to. As mentioned previously, Oppenheimer (1972) likens this to sightseeing, where tourists visit a complex environment and select items of interest. Unless one devises ways to change the nature of the informal environment by structuring the learning experiences, there is no reason to expect that a typical visitor should be able to recall specific information. There are only a few natural conditions with enough structure to make the measurement of recall an appropriate methodology for informal learning environments (see also Loftus, Levidow, & Duening 1992; MacManus 1993). For example, you might expect to find high levels of recall under the following conditions:

- The evaluator first observes the visitor interacting with a specific exhibit, and the participant manipulates the exhibit correctly, reads the labels aloud, or makes a specific comment that refers to the content of a label.
- The participant is a member of the museum staff or volunteers that have been specifically trained to help the public understand the exhibits, by giving tours or programs that emphasize the content of the exhibit.

- The evaluator sets up an experiment in which the visitor is asked to read a label or interact with an exhibit and then asked its meaning.

Klein (1981) suggests that the recognition of information is a more sensitive measure of retention and is more easily elicited. Recognition is more easily measured in informal learning environments, although it, too, has limitations. Sighted visitors store vast amounts of information as visual images that are collected as they wander through a museum, zoo, or aquarium. The most useful recognition tests, therefore, are visual based, measuring what subjects remember having seen in the course of a visit. On the other hand, text-based information presented in labels may be accessed by a more limited group of visitors. For example, in family groups, it is sometimes more common for an adult to read the labels (e.g., Diamond 1980; 1986; Ellenbogen, Luke, & Dierking 2004; McManus 1989a, b). These are frequently read aloud to other members of the group, with the result that younger children, in particular, usually hear labels rather than read them (see also Ash 2004; Borun, Chambers, & Cleghorn 1996; Crowley et al. 2001). Therefore, the best tests of recognition of text-based information may be those in which the text is read aloud to the participants. Recognition tests that require reading are the less preferred mode for studies of young children in informal learning environments.

Questions can be designed to measure either recall or recognition. Recall tests require participants to come up with specific information. On the other hand, to measure recognition, one might use a multiple-choice question, being sure to verify that the subjects understood the words used as alternatives in the answer. The following examples show how questions can be written to measure either recall or recognition. Questions that test recall:

What is a dinosaur? _____

A dinosaur is _____

Define *dinosaur*. _____

Question that tests recognition:

Check which of the following is true of dinosaurs:

1. Reptile
2. Extinct
3. A kind of animal
4. Amphibian
5. Living today

Another possibility is to have the participants look at pictures or models of different kinds of animals. Each subject would be asked to sort the dinosaurs from those that are not. It is helpful to clarify the participant's answer by asking "Why?" after they tell you which picture or model is a dinosaur.

If multiple-choice questions are too obvious and easy, then the participant will be able to figure them out without the help of the museum or zoo experience. If they are too detailed and difficult, no amount of informal learning will help the participant answer the questions. The choices need to be appropriate for the type of institution and for the age level of the audience being tested:

> The weakest aspect of multiple-choice forms is the difficulty in constructing good items. Often the correct answer can be guessed fairly easily because the distracters are so obviously wrong. . . . Trying out the initial test items on a sample of visitors for whom the test is intended does this. [Miles et al. 1988, p. 163]

MEASURING IMPLICIT MEMORY

Not all learning concerns information that we can consciously describe. For example, consider what knowledge a child acquires when he or she learns to ride a bike. Quite a bit of learning must occur; the child needs to get a sense of the relation between motion and balance, when and how to peddle to speed up and use the brakes to slow down, and how to use the handlebars when turning. At an intuitive and unconscious level, the child is actually learning some important principles of mechanics, such as torque and gear ratios. But very little of this information can be explicitly taught, in part because the potential teacher does not have conscious access to this knowledge. A parent or sibling might give the child some suggestions, but nothing can substitute for the feeling of knowing how to move and keep one's balance. Likewise, imagine how hard it is to teach someone to drive. The experienced driver knows precisely when and how to adjust speed, turn, or brake, but she or he finds that this knowledge is not easily described.

Cognitive scientists call this sort of knowledge *implicit memory* (Roediger 1990). Implicit memory includes all the knowledge that we possess but are not consciously aware of exactly what we know. We are often not aware of what we have learned. For instance, the child in the previous example cannot describe, and is probably not even aware of, the complex principles of balance, force, and torque that he or she mastered when learning to ride the bike. But clearly he or she learned something important. Even profound amnesiacs (i.e., people who have lost the ability to learn new facts or other explicit knowledge) often still possess implicit memory.

Implicit learning probably plays an important role in the museum experience. For example, a child visiting a science museum might learn the workings of a machine. She or he might not be able to label the parts of the machine or to state how gears work. Nevertheless, the child may have acquired a lot of information that could guide her or his future learning and museum visits. For example, the child might now be better able to learn about related machines, and his or her attention might be drawn to similar exhibits. Thus, the initial learning that occurred was in part implicit, in that the child was not consciously aware of what he or she had learned. It is possible that much of what visitors learn in informal institutions is implicit.

Measuring and studying implicit learning presents a special challenge: The fact that it is implicit means that we cannot simply ask people about their implicit knowledge. But there are some clever techniques for studying implicit memory. One involves what they call *priming* (Tulving & Schacter 1990). This technique is based on a simple idea: What we already know can affect how we learn or interpret new information. The priming technique involves having participants make judgments about information and assessing whether what they have learned previously affects the speed or accuracy of these judgments. The evaluator presents words or pictures that can elicit associations. For example, the evaluator might first present a picture of a table. The participant would be asked to make a simple judgment, such as deciding whether a picture was a piece of furniture. If primed with table, participants may be faster to make the judgments about chairs, but not about sofas or beds. The speed of the judgment is influenced by the prior-learned association between tables and chairs, even though the participant is not aware that this knowledge is influencing his or her judgments. What is important here is the demonstration that the participant's judgments are affected by the known relation between tables and chairs, even though the participant may not be aware that this relation affects his or her judgment.

Similar techniques could be applied to the study of informal learning. Does reminding people about an exhibit affect how they approach a new exhibit? If it does, then we have evidence that implicit learning has occurred; the prior exhibit affects their approach to the new exhibit. Moreover, we can be more detailed and specific about which elements of the prior exhibit affect learning in a new exhibit. We could, for example, show photographs of only portions of the prior exhibit to determine which aspects of the prior exhibit led to the most implicit learning.

In summary, much of what we know is implicit—we do not know that we know it. Implicit knowledge may be particularly important in informal learning, and measuring implicit knowledge can be an important skill for evaluators.

ASSESSING CONCEPTUAL CHANGE

Informal learning can extend far beyond the simple acquisition of facts and implicit knowledge. Museum designers sometimes hope to engender in their visitors deeper, more substantive changes in *how* visitors think about knowledge. Museum designers may want to help visitors understand the molecular basis of matter or the role of genetic variation in natural selection and evolution. Discovering that matter is made up of tiny particles and that its structure is governed by the properties and behavior of these particles can lead to a radical reorganization about how students view solids, liquids, and gases. They now can explain physical interactions in terms of these unobservable but extremely important bits of matter. They are thus relying on a different set of concepts (or theory) of the properties of matter than before they learned this information. This kind of knowledge transformation is not easily described in terms of a simple set of facts, and hence it cannot be easily assessed with measures of knowledge retention. Instead, cognitive scientists refer to the acquisition of this kind of knowledge as *conceptual change*. Conceptual change lies at the heart of much science learning, scientific discovery, and cognitive development (Carey 1997). Effective museum design therefore often will involve thinking about how to engender conceptual change.

Designing for conceptual change leads to the question of how it can be measured. How do we know when conceptual change has taken place? It is often not enough simply to ask visitors to recall facts or even to explain their concepts. Instead, we need to ask probing questions that require the participant to rely on his or her conceptual knowledge. One classic method for doing this is through *clinical interview*.

Clinical Interview

The clinical interview method is useful for assessing concepts and conceptual change. Jean Piaget, the Swiss biologist and developmental psychologist, provided detailed descriptions of how internal mental processes change as a result of the individual's experience with the world (Piaget 1973; Piaget & Inhelder 1969). He believed that learning occurred through the development of schemata in relation to new experiences. Piaget developed a form of interview, called the *task-based clinical interview*, in which subjects interact with objects and are asked detailed questions about their understanding of those objects. The evaluator leads the subject through a set of activities or problems, while being guided by the subject's own approach. Ackerman (1988) emphasizes that is easier to point out what researchers should not do. They should never try to suggest the right answers to the subject, and they should not compare the subject's performance to others. The purpose is not to define a correct or an incorrect method for interacting with objects or solving the problem:

> the purpose . . . is to uncover the originality of the child's reasoning, to rigorously describe its coherence and to probe its robustness or fragility in a variety of contexts. [Ackerman 1988, p. 10]

Elsa Feher has used this interview technique to examine how children acquire an understanding of concepts in a science center (Feher 1990; Feher & Meyer 1992):

> The interviewer, much like an anthropologist in the field, stations [himself or] herself at the chosen exhibit to conduct what is generally a small number of in-depth interviews. When a child approaches and starts investigating the exhibit, the interviewer engages the child in dialogue using questions from a protocol. The protocol is developed from a large number of preliminary test interviews, to ensure that the wording, content, and sequencing of the questions yield the best possible information. The questions ask for predictions and explanations of the phenomena that occur when the subject carries out specified tasks at the exhibit, e.g. "What will happen if you do such and such?" and "How can you explain what happened? Can you draw it?" The intuitive notions that the researchers collect are not simply ad hoc postulates advanced by the children to explain an isolated event. They are ideas organized into full-fledged models that allow for consistent predictions across several different tasks. [Feher 1990, p. 37]

To gain access to what Ackerman (1988) calls "deep theories," the clinician varies the constraints of the situation and then invites the participant to make guesses (e.g., What do you think will happen?). The participant is asked to express the guesses in various ways and then probe the guesses experimentally (e.g., Let's try . . .). The participant is asked to explain why a given guess was confirmed or not (e.g., What actually happened? Did you expect this to happen?) and is then asked to propose counter suggestions. The child may then be asked to explain his or her views, sometimes to another child.

Feher and Meyer (1992) used an exhibit about light to probe children's theories about color. One exhibit, called *Street Lights*, consists of different types of lamps used in street illumination, including a low-pressure sodium lamp and an incandescent lamp. Visitors can pick up colored objects, walk under the lights, and notice the variation in the objects' apparent color. Because the sodium lamp emits only yellow light, any object held under it will be seen as yellow if its pigments reflect yellow light, or it will look black if its pigments absorb yellow light. The other exhibit, called *Primary Lights*, consists of a small darkened room with red, green, and blue lights opposite a large, white screen. The visitor can control the lights, turning them off or on independently, and then observe the effects of mixing the colored light in various ways.

Feher and Meyer first asked 8–13-year-olds to look through a diffraction grating at the white light and then at the sodium light. Then they were asked to look at the colors in the panel drawings under the white light and to predict what they would look like under the sodium lamp. Finally, the children were asked to take crayons, write their names in various colors, and then predict what their names would look like under the two different kinds of light.

The authors proceeded through a series of questions, asking the children for their predictions, and then letting the children produce an effect on the exhibit. If the effect did not match the children's predictions, then they were asked to provide an explanation. It is these explanations that provide the material from which the children's fundamental understanding and the mental rules that they use for explaining how things work are modeled (Table 3.1). In this way, when the clinical interview method is used with interactive exhibits, it becomes a powerful tool for understanding how people think in informal educational settings. Using similar techniques, Jee et al. (2015) conducted clinical interviews to compare student, teacher, and virologist's understanding of viruses and infectious disease.

Table 3.1 Results of a clinical interview method used as a means of eliciting children's understanding of phenomena in exhibits at the Reuben Fleet Space Theater and Science Center.

Type	Example Responses (n = 34)	Frequency
The shadow is dark or black.	"The light is hitting it [ball], and the shadow will hit the screen, and it will be dark." "When the light is hitting the ball it [light] doesn't make any color, the ball makes the shadow." "The ball stops the light, it's not the color red anymore and the shadow goes to the wall." "It'll be dark, black because it [ball] is blocking the light."	59%
The shadow is the color of the light.	"The light is red and it's reflecting off the ball. It is bouncing off the ball." "With red light the shadow is red; when you're outside the shadow looks black because the sun's hitting it instead of red."	35%
The shadow is the color of the object.	"Green, because the tennis ball is green."	6%

Children aged from eight to thirteen were interviewed at Primary Lights, which consisted of a small, dark room with a red, green, and white light opposite a large white screen. They were asked to explain the effects of blocking the various lights with a tennis ball. In one part of the study, the children were told, "Hold this ball here [between the light and the screen]. If I turn on this red light, what will you see on the screen?" This table shows the frequency of responses of the subjects' predictions (Feher & Meyer 1992:514). Reprinted with permission of John Wiley & Sons, Inc.

Conceptual Change about Evolution

Evans and her colleagues studied how the *Explore Evolution* exhibit influenced visitors' understanding (Diamond & Evans 2007; Diamond, Evans, & Spiegel 2012). They investigated how museum visitors reason about evolution before, during, and after visits to the *Explore Evolution* exhibits (see Figure 3.1). The exhibit and related educational materials served as devices for eliciting people's thinking patterns, which were then analyzed for evidence of conceptual change.

To understand visitors' reasoning before they came to the exhibit, Evans focused on the commonsense explanations or intuitive theories that inform children's and adults' everyday understanding of the world. She began by asking adult natural history museum visitors open-ended questions about the evolutionary problems to be presented in the exhibition (Evans et al. 2009; Spiegel et al. 2012). She and her colleagues then did an exhaustive coding of visitors' responses into explanations from evolutionary, creationist, and intuitive reasoning patterns. From the 32 adult visitors' responses, over 600 distinct relevant codes were identified.

On the basis of their responses to the evolutionary problems, visitors were categorized into three types of reasoning patterns. Visitors that used intuitive

Figure 3.1 A young visitor at the Explore Evolution exhibit measures the bills of medium ground finches from the Galapagos to see variations in their size.

reasoning were categorized as using *novice naturalistic reasoning* (Table 3.2). Visitors who had a basic grasp of Darwinian evolutionary explanations, though they were not experts, were categorized as using *informed naturalistic reasoning*. Visitors that invoked supernatural explanations used *creationist reasoning*. Subsumed under each of these three reasoning patterns were a number of themes that referenced concepts judged to be characteristic of that particular pattern. For example, visitors using the informed naturalistic reasoning pattern might reference one or more of the evolutionary principles of variation, inheritance, selection, and time that provided the conceptual framework for the exhibit (Figure 3.2).

Table 3.2   Evans and her colleagues presented problems to visitors to elicit their reasoning patterns about evolution (Evans et al. 2009).

Fruit fly problem:	**Informed naturalistic reasoning**
Visitors were asked, Scientists think that about 8 million years ago a couple of fruit flies managed to land on an Hawaiian island. Before that time, there were no fruit flies in Hawaii (show map). Now scientists have found that there are 800 different kinds of fruit flies in Hawaii. How do you explain this?	In this example, the visitor invoked several evolutionary concepts, though the visitor was clearly not an expert:

In this example, the visitor invoked several evolutionary concepts, though the visitor was clearly not an expert:

> *Well, the process of evolution. So, at certain points there were, uh, mutations that just naturally occurred. Um, . . . reproduction. And then, those mutations, if they were adapted to that environment, they were further reproduced, and if they were not adapted, the mutations just ceased—those fruit flies died off. So that would explain the variety.*

Novice naturalistic reasoning

In this example, intuitive modes of reasoning are invoked, which indicate that the visitor is not conceptualizing this problem as one of evolutionary change:

> *Obviously people have brought the fruit flies in. And Dole probably, Dole pineapple people probably brought them in.*

Creationist reasoning

This visitor invoked supernatural rather than natural explanations, in particular, God's direct role in the origin of species:

> *Um, first of all I have a problem with your 8 million years. I believe in creation in the biblical account, so that pretty well defines how I believe things. God created them and due to the great flood, that is how the diversity came and that would be my explanation. . . Ok, I believe um, God created a pair, a male and female of everything with the ability to diversify. So I guess what I meant at the time of the flood, I believe that's when the continents broke apart and so even though only a few of each things were saved in the flood, they had the genetic background to be able to diversify into all of the, like for instance, dogs, and all the different kinds that we have. And so um, does that help? Just a creationistic view.*

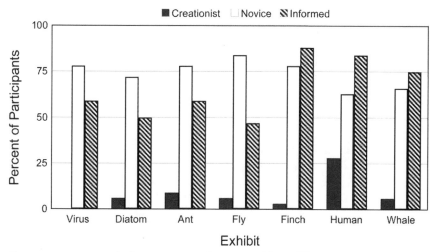

Figure 3.2 An example from Evans et al. (2009) of how different visitors' reasoning patterns varied for the seven different organisms presented in an evolution exhibit.

From an analysis of the visitors' responses, Evans and her colleagues developed a questionnaire to assess conceptual change. Sixty-two adults and youth were recruited to take part in a typical gallery visit to the exhibit. Before the visit, they were given four of the seven evolutionary problems in a questionnaire format. Following the visit, they were asked about all seven problems, three open-ended questions, and detailed demographic questions that probed their religious beliefs, attitudes toward evolution, and interest in the exhibit.

What did they find? A single visit to the *Explore Evolution* exhibit improved visitors' abilities to explain evolutionary problems, and this improvement was seen across participants (Evans et al. 2009). Moreover, visitors realized that evolution occurred regardless of the nature of the organism. The investigations of evolution in seven diverse organisms in the exhibit helped visitors to understand that evolution occurs in all living things.

TASK ANALYSIS AND THINK-ALOUD PROTOCOLS

Sometimes, it is useful to ask a subject to recall exactly how they performed a task or engaged in an activity. It is not a simple process to elicit this kind of information, because many participants do not know how to remember that much detail about a previous activity. Moreover, participants can show substantial biases when they are asked to think about whether or how they learned something.

Researchers have used *task analysis* as a way of gathering details on the cognitive processes involved in physical tasks. This method is a feature of information-processing psychology, and its goal is to understand how people think while doing complex tasks. Based on a series of interviews, a subject's thinking processes are modeled schematically, noting the steps that people take, in what order they take them, and the errors they make. The models, and ultimately the steps in the thinking process, may then be replicated in a computer program.

According to Larkin and Rainard (1984), the procedure begins when a subject is simply asked to do a task and to talk aloud about all thoughts that occur. These comments are tape-recorded and transcribed to a formal record called a *protocol*:

> A protocol is simply a list of verbal statements made by the problem solver. A protocol is not a complete record of the solver's thoughts nor does it tell why the solver does what he does. The solver does not mention every thought that goes through his [or her] head, and protocol statements rarely show why the solver does something. The protocol just provides regular indications of what the solver is thinking. From them the researcher must infer a more complete model of the entire problem solving process. [Larkin & Rainard 1984, p. 236]

When a protocol is complete, the next step is to build a process model of the task of interest. The process model includes the representation of the solver's knowledge about the problem, the rules that describe what the solver does as he or she develops the problem representation, and an interpreter who matches the conditions of the rules against the problem representation. The interpreter produces a series of condition-action rules for building problem representations. Each rule describes an action, together with the conditions under which it is possible and useful to use this action. Each action is a change in the problem representation. When these condition-action rules are then written into computer program, it becomes a way of testing the problem representation. The computer program verifies whether the condition-action rules are sufficient to solve the problem of interest. In this way, according to Larkin and Rainard (1984), the model solutions are compared to the human solutions to show whether the model provides a good account of what human solvers do. Larkin (1989) used task analysis to model how subjects solve problems that involve everyday tasks. In one study, she modeled the cognitive processes involved in making a cup of coffee. Invariably, even simple tasks are much more complicated than one might expect.

A detailed record of the steps involved in performing a task or solving a problem can be a useful guide for informal educational environments. Exhibits frequently have written labels that direct visitors' actions to perform a task, after which the visitors are requested to observe some effect or change.

What might at first appear to be a simple series of actions is not always so, and a task analysis can provide an accurate description of the required steps. Larkin and Rainard (1984) emphasize that the techniques of information-processing psychology are most useful where it is important, not just whether individuals can do a certain task, but also how they are doing this task. In a museum, park, or zoo, when visitors continue to find a task incomprehensible despite the best efforts at teaching it, this kind of study can show what prevents them from learning.

MEASURING VISUAL-SPATIAL MEMORY

Not all of the information that people store in their minds is coded as words. Cognitive maps refer to the way a person's brain represents or stores certain visual information. The picture that is stored is not necessarily a correct one, but it guides how people move through environments, how they chose new stimuli, and ultimately how they mentally process new experiences. Lazlo and his colleagues (1996) describe such mental maps as the following:

> Cognitive maps are mental representations of the worlds in which we live. They are built of our individual experience, recorded as memories and tested against the unceasing demands of reality. These maps, however, do not simply represent the worlds of our experience in a passive and unchanging way. They are, in fact, dynamic models of the environments in which we carry out our daily lives, and as such determine much of what we expect, and even what we see. Thus, they represent and at the same time participate in the creation of our individual realities. [Lazlo, Artigiani, Combs, & Csányi 1996, p. 3]

First described by the psychologist Edward Tolman in the 1940s, the study of cognitive maps has become a tool in understanding the relationship between an organism and its environment. According to Gallistel (1990) a cognitive map is a record in the central nervous system of macroscopic geometric relations among surfaces in an environment and is used to plan movements through the environment. The relationship between the record in the nervous system and a person's movements may be anything but literal. Pick (1993) emphasizes that even children may have complex configurational knowledge that guides their movements. For example, children have been shown to reconstruct spatial layouts more accurately if they had walked around the periphery than after they had walked within the space. They were most accurate when they had walked within the space and their attention was called to the spatial relations.

In this way, a cognitive map may be like a pictorial representation. Spatial elements that are understandable and thus familiar in some sense may be

presented on the map. Elements that are unfamiliar may be distorted, omit-
ted, or translated in some manner. The cognitive map encodes a person's
understanding and familiarity with an environment, leaving gaps for images
that are not understood.

The way that we remember the location of a place is not exactly the same
way it is represented in a physical map. We might remember key items at
particular locations, such as a stop sign at a corner, a large church, or a park,
and then use these items to guide our recall of how to navigate there. Large-
scale features are used to set a course that brings one into the vicinity of a
sought-for-place and then attention may be shifted to local cues. In general,
the way people (and other animals) respond to the spatial configurations of a
familiar environment is generally based not on immediate sensory input from
the environment but rather on their internal map and their perceived position
on the map.

The first time that someone visits a museum, zoo, or aquarium, they create
an internal representation of that experience, and subsequent visits will lead
to modifications in the internal representation. How visitors explore the environment, however, and what they ultimately pay attention to, will be largely
guided by the internal map. The way that people configure a cognitive map
can provide clues to the features of the environment that are important and
that may ultimately have resilience in memory. A person's later drawings of
the exhibit or gallery can provide clues to the meaning of that experience for
that individual (Figure 3.3). This can provide a means for accessing visual
memories without having to first rely on verbal reporting of them. When possible, a subject should try to provide verbal descriptions of their drawing to
explain features that may not be apparent.

One needs to be cautious in interpreting cognitive maps, particularly when
using drawings. According to Kosslyn, Heldmeyer, and Locklear (1980), a
subject's verbal interpretations are as important as actual drawings. Maps
are not fixed features, so they may change dramatically from one time to the
next. More important experiences may be represented larger than life, or in
relatively greater detail than other events, but this is not always so. Finally,
subjects vary in their ability to produce various kinds of memory maps.
In fact, if a subject has been trained to draw, they may rely to a greater extent
on preexisting rules for recreating visual scenes and to a lesser extent on their
mental images.

THE TIME FRAME OF LEARNING ASSESSMENT

Thus far, we have discussed different methods for assessing different kinds of
learning. But regardless of the measures that they use, all informal evaluators

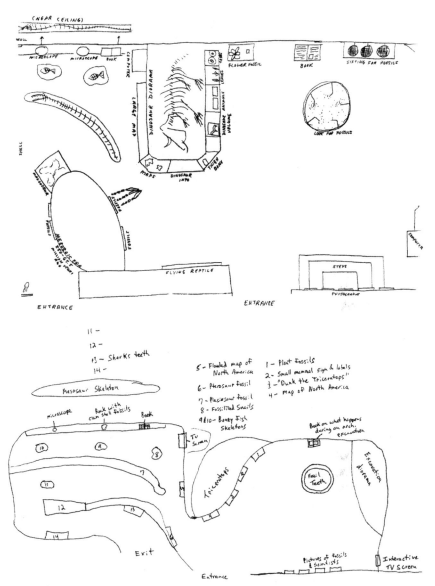

Figure 3.3 Graduate students in a museum studies program visited the NSF-funded Mesozoic Gallery at the University of Nebraska State Museum and later created drawings of the gallery from memory.

and researchers face the challenge of deciding when to administer a measure of learning. Should we measure learning while it is happening—during the visit—or should we wait to see how much information visitors retain?

Many researchers measure visitors' knowledge both before and after their visits. This design is known as a *pretest–posttest design*. The variable to be tested for differences should be one that is likely to be influenced by the exhibit or program. Typically, subjects are given a test of some sort before they go into the exhibit, and then they are retested after they leave that particular gallery. Differences in the two tests may be attributed to the effects of the exhibit. Another common method is a posttest-only design, where subjects randomly assigned to one of two groups that are compared on their test performance.

Pretest–posttest measures can provide rigorous assessments of learning. But in the freewheeling informal environment, pretest–posttest design (or posttest-only designs) presents special challenges. Because visitors are not necessarily directed to pay attention to specific elements, it is not obvious as to which features of the environment one should test. Invariably, when a pretest is introduced into this environment, it signals the users to pay particular attention to the variables the test contains. The results of the pretest–posttest design may suggest impacts of the gallery, but these impacts may only be relevant for the condition of the test, when users are directed to particular aspects of the exhibit. The posttest-only design assumes that all of the subjects will be exposed to the same features of the environment. Because informal environments involve a free choice of features, it is not typical for everyone to see or do the same thing. These experimental designs are less likely to provide information on what the typical visitor learns in the museum, zoo, or park, so as to inform us about what visitors are capable of learning, when they are so directed.

One way to deal with the effect of a pretest on visitor's experiences and learning is to arrange for a control group or a comparison group. By including a comparison group, the researcher can get some traction on whether the museum exhibit of interest is having the intended effect. We might expect, for example, that visitors in a control group, who do not experience the exhibit that we are studying, would learn less than a group that does experience the exhibit. In these cases, participants are randomly assigned to one or more experimental groups or to a control group. Each group is given the pretest. Each experimental group may, for example, be exposed to a different program format (e.g., acting out events versus handling objects). The control group is not exposed to the program; they may be allowed to roam freely through the museum. Then all groups are given the posttest. Measurement of the differences between the tests in the groups can provide insight into which kind of program or free time was more effective at teaching the concepts measured on the test. A general rule for this model is to make the pretest and posttest questions realistic indicators of what people are expected to learn in a museum. For example, they should not rely heavily on detailed factual information that might be contained in exhibit labels. Rather, the questions should ask about the subject's experience with or attitudes toward the phenomena demonstrated by the exhibits.

Pretests and posttests should be used cautiously in informal settings. In general, the pretest–posttest model tends to de-emphasize more significant informal learning experiences in favor of simple kinds of text-based information. Conceptual change in informal settings is often gradual, and people rarely spend time reflecting on or synthesizing their experiences. It may take days, weeks, or even months for the informal educational experience to be sufficiently integrated with prior knowledge for significant learning to be measurable. This provides a special challenge when we attempt to measure learning in informal settings. Although visitors may have experienced a great deal, they often take days or weeks to integrate their new experiences into a conceptual framework.

Roschelle (1995) suggests the kinds of general questions that should reflect a more accurate nature of informal learning. For example, do museums, zoos, or parks raise visitors' awareness of alternative perspectives? Do visitors formulate personally relevant questions? Do visitors realize how they can tap their current knowledge to enter a new field of inquiry? Do the informal institutions provide models of constructive learning processes with which visitors can go on learning? Do visitors become aware of books, videos, and other resources that start from what they know already? Are informal institutions a place where visitors can use prior knowledge to help their friends and family learn? Do these institutions provide a setting for integrating diverse views that comprise a rich understanding?

From these general questions, one needs to focus on specific issues. How does your experience with this exhibit relate to anything you have done outside the museum? What kinds of questions does this particular exhibit make you think of? How does this exhibit relate to books, videos, or other resources you know of? What would you tell a child about the exhibit you have just seen?

Chapter 4

Protecting Study Participants

PROTECTING PARTICIPANTS' RIGHTS

Researchers and evaluators have ethical and legal obligations to protect the rights of study participants. This obligation is important regardless of where the research takes place. Because informal learning institutions are generally public environments, it can be easy to gather data about people without them being aware of what is occurring. Study subjects, however, should always be given sufficient knowledge of an evaluation or other research project to make an informed decision about whether they want to participate. Most studies in informal settings involve minimal risk, meaning that the potential harm resulting from participation in the study is not greater than that encountered in daily life. However, participants still have a right to be well informed about the nature of the study and its possible consequences.

Guidelines for the protection of research participants were first codified at the end of World War II during the Nuremberg War Crime Trials. These guidelines, called the *Nuremberg Code*, were drafted as a set of standards for judging scientists who had conducted medical experiments on concentration camp prisoners. The code served as a basis for subsequent efforts to create ethical guidelines for conducting research. In 1974, when the National Research Act was signed into law, a commission was created to identify the basic ethical principles that should underlie the conduct of all biomedical and behavioral research involving human participants. The commission developed guidelines that should be followed to assure that such research is conducted in accordance with the principles. In 1979, the commission created the *Belmont Report* (Department of Health, Education and Welfare 1979), which was soon adopted as federal policy. Currently, this federal policy is known as the *Code of Federal Regulations, Part 46 Protection of Human Subjects*, or more frequently, the "Common Rule."

INSTITUTIONAL REVIEW BOARDS

Research studies that are designed to be systematic and generalizable need to comply with the *Belmont Report* and more recent federal guidelines for protecting the rights of research participants, such as the Common Rule. Compliance is assessed on a case-by-case basis by a committee called *Institutional Review Board* (IRB). These committees review research plans that involve human participants. A central element of the review is the concept of *informed consent*, which describes how participants are informed about all of the possible impacts of participating in the research. Participants must also fully understand their right not to participate in the research—they need to know that they can walk away at any time, and they should never be coerced into participating. Typically, an investigator submits an overview of a research project, with specific details on how participants will be informed about their rights. The IRB then reviews the information and ultimately gives permission before the study can proceed.

How do you know if you need to submit your study to an IRB for review? Do informal evaluators need to go through the IRB process to achieve compliance with the legal and ethical guidelines laid out to protect human research participants? Federal guidelines define research as a systematic investigation designed to develop or contribute to generalizable knowledge. Evaluation, however, is sometimes designed not to advance generalizable knowledge but rather to provide context-specific information. Universities and federal agencies such as the National Science Foundation often require evaluators to seek IRB compliance, especially for studies in which the results are applicable beyond a single context. Thus, evaluators are wise to submit their evaluation plan to an IRB for review, or at least discuss them with an IRB staff member, so that an informed decision can be made about whether the study is IRB exempt.

Although universities have IRBs that will review both faculty and student research plans, many informal education institutions do not have any established process to ensure that their visitors are adequately protected. How do evaluators not affiliated with a university find an IRB who will review their plans and give permission for implementation of the study? Private IRB companies will shepherd researchers and evaluators through the process and, for a fee, provide access to a legitimate committee that will review study plans. The National Science Foundation disseminates a list of potential private IRBs.

In working with any IRB, either university based or private, it is important to remember the following:

- Talk with someone at the IRB office before you submit your application. Explain your situation and ask for their advice regarding any issues or

materials of which you are unsure. For example, if you think your project is exempt, call one of the IRB staff members and talk it over. Most IRBs encourage these kinds of conversations, and they can be helpful.
- Provide as much context as possible in your evaluation plan. IRB committee members will not be familiar with designing or conducting studies in informal learning settings. For instance, do not assume that they will understand how one recruits participants in a public setting.
- Make sure you have an IRB training certificate. Most IRBs now require that the study investigators have an up-to-date training certification, demonstrating an understanding of the various issues and procedures related to protecting human research participants. The National Institutes of Health (NIH) offers an online training program through their Office of Human Subjects Research, as does the University of Miami through their Collaborative Institutional Training Initiative (https://www.citiprogram.org).

INFORMED CONSENT

The legal standard of informed consent requires that prospective participants be provided with the following information (University of Nebraska-Lincoln Institutional Review Board 2015):

- A general description of the research, including the purpose for which it is being performed, the duration for which the participant is expected to participate, the procedures to be followed, and the exact nature of any procedures that are experimental.
- An account of any potential risks or discomforts to the participant. A description of any benefits to the participants or others that may be reasonably expected from the research.
- A commitment to maintenance of confidentiality in subject records and a description as to how confidentiality will be maintained.
- A statement of the participant's right to ask questions and to have those questions answered, and the name and phone number of people to contact for answers to any questions about the research. This includes questions about the rights of research participants.
- A statement that participation is voluntary, that refusal to participate will involve no penalty or loss of benefits to which the participant is otherwise entitled, and that the subject may discontinue participation at any time without loss of benefits to which the participant is otherwise entitled.

If you think that participation in the study might involve more than minimal risk, you should include an explanation of any compensation that is offered, as well as whether medical treatment is available should an injury occur, what that treatment consists of, and where further information may be obtained.

Some participants require special protection, because they may not be able to make informed decisions about their participation in the study. Special care needs to be taken to ensure the rights of children and other individuals who lack self-determination. This may include people subject to illness, disability, or other circumstances that may restrict freedom of choice.

One of the possible consequences of following ethical guidelines is that fully informing participants about their participation in a study may result in altering their behavior or opinions during the research. If the process of obtaining informed consent has been carefully conducted, however, the impacts of knowing about the study are likely to be small. Nevertheless, if the evaluator thinks that the research process has influenced the outcome of the study, it is important that this be considered when generalizations are made from the study results.

Honesty and openness in the presentation of the study will make the project appear less threatening. Sometimes participants mistakenly believe that the purpose of the study is to make judgments about their performance. It can be reassuring to them to know that the purpose is to make improvements in the institution or its programs. For examples of consent forms, see Figures 4.1 and 4.2.

IRB# 20110311649EP
Date Approved: 02/27/2012
Valid Until: 03/14/2013

Youth Assent Form

World of Viruses Study

We want to invite you to take part in this study. You are being asked because you are in a biology science class.

World of Viruses is a project to help teach about viruses. This project will produce different materials, including essays and comics and other educational materials for youth and adults. To make these materials as interesting and helpful as they can be, we want to get some feedback from you about them. Your answers will help us make these materials more useful and interesting to students your age.

There are no known risks to you in answering the questions, and you may find reading the materials and answering the questions interesting.

Participation in this study will take place in your classroom and take about one class period. You will be randomly assigned to read one of four different reading materials and asked to complete a survey after reading. You will not give your name and there is no way for us to know which answers belong to you or someone else. Your grade in this class will not be affected in any way by your participation in this study.

You do not have to be in this study if you do not want to, and you may skip questions or stop answering at any time. If you choose not to participate, your teacher will provide an alternative activity.

If you have a question at any time, please ask the teacher or the researcher in your classroom.

If you complete the survey, it means that you have decided to participate this research study and have read everything on this form. You are welcome to keep a copy of this form if you would like.

Thank you for helping us learn more about what you know about viruses!

Investigator Information:

Dr. Judy Diamond, University of Nebraska State Museum, jdiamond1@unl.edu or 402-472-4433
Dr. Amy Spiegel, Center for Instructional Innovation, aspiegel1@unl.edu or 402-472-0764

University of Nebraska-Lincoln Bureau of Sociological Research 301 Benton Hall 402-472-3672
For more information, contact Nicole Bryner or Amanda Richardson at 402-472-3672 or e-mail bosr@unl.edu

Figure 4.1   Child informed consent developed by Amy Spiegel at the Center for Instructional Innovation at the University of Nebraska for a study funded by the NIH SEPA program on the impacts of comics on science attitudes and interest (Spiegel et al. 2013).

TO: **PARENT/GUARDIAN**
FROM: University of Nebraska State Museum
SUBJECT: **PASSIVE CONSENT FORM** for the World of Viruses Study

Your son/daughter's science classroom is participating in the World of Viruses Study. The data gathered from this study will be used to help design better and more engaging materials for science education.

Students will take the survey during a regular class period in their classroom. Completing this survey poses no risk to your child and covers materials similar to what students learn in science class. Survey procedures have been designed to protect your child's privacy. Students do not put their names on the survey and no student or school will be mentioned by name in a report of the results.

For the study your child will be asked to read either an essay or a comic book with science information. After reading the essay or comic, each participating student will be asked to complete a short survey about the materials.

Student participation is encouraged and appreciated, but is completely voluntary. The data collected is extremely useful in the development of educational materials related to improving science interest and education for our youth. However, participation is voluntary and there are no consequences if a student does not participate, and student participation does not affect their grade in any way. Students who do not participate in the study will be given an alternate activity by the teacher. If for some reason you do not wish for your child to participate, please complete and return the form on the reverse of this letter.

The Bureau of Sociological Research (BOSR) at the University of Nebraska-Lincoln will be managing the survey administration for University of Nebraska State Museum. If there is any additional information you would find helpful or to see a copy of study materials, please contact Nicole Bryner or Amanda Richardson at bosr@unl.edu, or call 402-472-3672, and they will be happy to assist you.

University of Nebraska-Lincoln Bureau of Sociological Research 301 Benton Hall 402-472-3672
For more information, contact Nicole Bryner or Amanda Richardson at 402-472-3672 or e-mail bosr@unl.edu

Figure 4.2 Parent passive consent developed by Amy Spiegel at the Center for Instructional Innovation at the University of Nebraska for a study funded by the NIH SEPA program on the impacts of comics on science attitudes and interest (Spiegel et al. 2013).

World of Viruses Passive Consent Form

I have read the information about the **World of Viruses Study** being conducted by the University of Nebraska-Lincoln Museum. Please check the box below **only if you do not** want your son/daughter to take part in the survey.

| | My child does **not** have my permission to participate. |

Name of student_____ Grade_____

Signature of parent/guardian_____ Date_____

Please have your son/daughter return this form to his/her teacher within the next three days ONLY if you do not wish them to participate.

Thank you so much for your assistance with this important project.

Investigator Information:

Dr. Judy Diamond, University of Nebraska State Museum, jdiamond1@unl.edu or 402-472-4433
Dr. Amy Spiegel, Center for Instructional Innovation, aspiegel1@unl.edu or 402-472-0764

If you have questions or concerns about your rights as a study participant that have not been answered by the investigators, or to report any concerns about the project, please contact the University of Nebraska-Lincoln Institutional Review Board at 402-472-6965.

University of Nebraska-Lincoln Bureau of Sociological Research 301 Benton Hall 402-472-3672
For more information, contact Nicole Bryner or Amanda Richardson at 402-472-3672 or e-mail bosr@unl.edu

Figure 4.2   (continued)

Part II

EVALUATION TOOLS

There is ongoing interplay between evaluation questions and the methods used to answer those questions. In an idealized research study, one formulates questions and then selects the methods best suited to answer those questions. In practice, the interplay between questions and methods can be more bidirectional. Although choice of methods is typically directed by the nature of the research questions, consideration of methods will also determine what evaluation questions you can address.

A broad distinction in methods is whether they are quantitative or qualitative in nature. *Quantitative* methods attempt to classify diverse opinions or behaviors into established categories. These studies are designed to look for numerical patterns in data, summarizing reactions of many people to a limited set of variables. Quantitative methods often make comparisons between categories of data by using statistical tests to establish the nature of the relationships among variables. They may include experiments, tests, observations, surveys, or other means of comparing the responses or behavior of different groups. A primary advantage of quantitative methods is that they provide findings that can be generalized to larger populations.

Qualitative methods, on the other hand, emphasize the depth of understanding over how well they can be generalized to larger populations. These methods allow the evaluator to examine individual cases or events in depth and detail. They may emphasize overall trends, but they may also seek out exceptions, particularly how special cases differ from the mainstream. Qualitative methods utilize direct quotations, detailed reporting of events, interviews, and behavioral observations. Qualitative studies can be especially helpful when you are just starting to examine a problem and or when the important issues are not yet clear. They are also effective as a way of

43

describing complex or unpredictable phenomena that cannot be easily summarized into discrete categories.

Increasingly, evaluators are using quantitative and qualitative methods together, a so-called mixed-methods approach to evaluation. For example, a single evaluation study may use qualitative methods to generate ideas, categories, and questions, while at the same time, it uses quantitative methods to verify those results for a larger population. Together, the two approaches combine insight, depth, and an appreciation for differences with consistency, predictability, and the ability to generalize broadly.

The guiding principles of validity and reliability are important at this phase of an evaluation study. *Validity* refers to the notion that the measure or instrument you have developed is accurate and appropriate, given what you are trying to measure. If you are using a series of behaviors to determine whether learning has occurred, then you need to be sure that the behaviors are valid indicators of learning. For example, observing a visitor looking at a label is not necessarily evidence that they have read the label; to call it reading behavior would have poor validity. Validity is always an issue in evaluation, whether you are conducting observations, interviews, questionnaires, or tests. Basically, if the measures are consistent with outside experts' notions of what they should be measuring, then it is more likely to be valid.

Reliability is a measure of how consistent a method is. A reliable method measures the same thing, usually in the same way, each time it is used. Reliability is influenced by the method's precision (i.e., is it free from random errors?), by its sensitivity (i.e., does it respond to small changes?), and by its resolution (i.e., how small a difference will it notice?). For example, when conducting observations, a behavioral category that is poorly defined may not be reliable because it may indicate different behavior patterns each time it is used. A question in an interview that is asked a different way each time may not be reliable because it elicits a different kind of response depending on the way that it is asked.

In this section, we focus on methods for collecting data. Chapter 5 introduces issues of sampling, including how to select your sample, determine sample size, and gain access to study participants. Chapters 6 and 7 describe the key methods used by evaluators in informal learning environments, including tracking movements, observations, behavior sampling, informal conversational interviews, semi-structured and structured interviews, personal meaning mapping, questionnaire development, and web questionnaires. Chapter 8 provides step-by-step guidance on how to depict and analyze the data you collect, emphasizing both quantitative and qualitative methods.

Chapter 5

Selecting Study Participants

HOW MANY PARTICIPANTS?

How many participants should you include in your study? In statistics, a *sample* refers to a subset of a larger population. For example, in a survey study of museum visitors, you might collect a sample of 50 people that you intend to represent the much larger population of all possible visitors. The sample size and the sampling strategy impact the interpretation of your study results. If your sample has been carefully selected, then what holds true for the sample is more likely to be accurate for the entire population. Bias in sampling or too small a sample will skew the findings, so that information from the sample may not be generally true of the public at large.

The size of your sample depends on the purpose of your study and the methods you use. Quantitative methods require larger samples than do qualitative methods, because the purpose of the former is to generalize results from a sample of strategically selected people to a much larger audience. In this case, the sample size typically depends on the following:

- How important it is for your results to generalize beyond your study.
- The size and variability of the population of interest.
- The smallest subgroup within the population for which estimates are needed.

There are a few rules of thumb that can help you select the size of your sample:

- About five to ten participants may be useful for exploratory evaluations that raise questions to be pursued later. Focus groups may comfortably include

45

10 to 20 participants. Qualitative studies may sample participants from a variety of different subgroups to get as much variability as possible.
• About 40 to 60 individuals are required to provide a pool large enough for most kinds of quantitative analysis.
• If you expect that your groups will differ substantially in a quantitative study, then a smaller sample may be sufficient.
• In quantitative studies, think about your sample in terms of the number of groups you want to compare. Choose a sample that is large enough so that each group or "cell" in your analytical table contains at least ten participants. First create a dummy table with the participant groups listed on the left column and the analytical categories along the top (see Table 5.1).

How do you tell how large a sample of participants should be included in a study? In large part, it depends on the size of the larger population that your sample will represent. Table 5.2 shows the sample sizes needed for different sizes of populations. Note that as your population gets larger, eventually you reach a point where the size of the sample changes only little or not at all. Thus, if you can accept a 10 percent sampling error, and the museum has a million visitors each year, it is reasonable to make generalizations on the basis of a random sample of 96 visitors. This is the same sample size

Table 5.1   Example of a three-by-three design. If you have ten samples in each cell and nine cells, then the total number of subjects needed would be 10 × 9 = 90.

Grade	School A	School B	School C
K–2	10	10	10
3–5	10	10	10
6–8	10	10	10

Table 5.2   Sample size needed for different sizes of populations (adapted from Salant & Dillman 1994, p. 55). The sampling error is a measure of the potential error that occurs when researchers gather data from only a sample, instead of the entire population.

Population Size	+/– 3% Sampling Error	+/– 10% Sampling Error
100	92	49
500	341	81
1,000	516	88
5,000	880	94
10,000	964	95
50,000	1,045	96
100,000	1,056	96
1,000,000	1,066	96
100,000,000	1,067	96

that you would use if the museum had 50,000 visitors or 10 million visitors. It is more common to require a sampling error of 3 percent, and still there is only one more participant required for a population of 100 million than for a population of one million. This is why pollsters, who generally require a 3 percent sampling error, can make generalizations about a whole country's population based on a sample of only a few thousand. This works, however, only if the sample is not biased—and it very often is biased. We discuss more on avoiding bias below.

SELECTING PARTICIPANTS FOR QUANTITATIVE STUDIES

After establishing the desired sample size, the next step is to decide how to select participants. The method for selecting participants can differ depending on whether you use quantitative or qualitative methods. This section discusses how to select participants when using quantitative methods. Because the goal of such studies are to generalize results to a larger population, how you select the participants will have a bearing on how broadly you can generalize.

When you are studying a fairly small population (e.g., people who have taken classes at the museum), you may find that you are able to include all of the members of the population as participants. In this case, you are not really sampling from the population because you are able to include everybody that you are interested in studying. Most often, however, your population is too large to include every member in your study. In these cases, you have to sample a smaller group of participants that will give you an indication of how the larger population will respond.

Two common methods for sampling in quantitative studies are systematic and representational sampling. In *systematic sampling*, participants are selected so that there are equivalent numbers from each group (Table 5.3). Systematic sampling lends itself to some kinds of statistical analysis in which it is desirable to have an equal sample size in each category. Table 5.3 is an example of systematic sampling for gender and age. Half of the subjects in each age group would be male and the other half would be female. Half of the subjects of each gender would be adults and the rest would be children.

Sometimes you want to select your participants on the basis of how frequently individuals with specific demographic characteristics appear in the

Table 5.3 An example of systematic sampling for gender and age.

	Females	Males
Adults	20	20
Children	20	20

Table 5.4 An example of representational sampling for ethnicity.

	Hispanic (%)	African American (%)	Caucasian (%)	Asian (%)	Pacific Islander (%)	American Indian (%)	Others (%)
Adults and children	50	10	20	10	3	4	3

overall population. This is called *representational sampling*. This sampling determines sample sizes of each category in proportion to its frequency in the population of interest (Table 5.4). If you are selecting participants by their ethnic group or age, you may want to select group members by how frequently they appear in the museum population. For example, if senior citizens make up 60 percent of your audience, children make up 20 percent, and non-senior adults make up the other 20 percent, you may want to select your sample according to these percentages.

Table 5.4 is an example of representational sampling for ethnicity. If your total sample size is 100, and the larger population in your region consists of 50 percent Hispanic, 10 percent African Americans, 20 percent Caucasian, 10 percent Asian, 3 percent Pacific Islander, 4 percent American Indian, and 3 percent other ethnic groups, then a representational sample would be as shown in the table.

Whether you use systematic or representational sampling, the next step is to decide how to select which individuals will be included in your sample. You need some way of ensuring that any member of the population has an equal chance of being included in your sample. It is important that you do not choose your participants on the basis of some other, possibly biased criteria (e.g., participants who look friendly or those who speak to you first). One practical method is to set up a system for alternating your choices: If you are sampling female and male adults, you can choose the first female that walks in the door and ask her to participate. If she agrees, then you return to the door, and select the next male who walks in and then agrees to participate. Some researchers advocate choosing the fifth subject from each category who appears at the designated selection location; this can be useful when there are large numbers of visitors entering at the same time.

The method of alternating choices is acceptable when the likelihood of each participant entering the building is about the same. However, when you want to systematically sample by age or ethnicity, and some classes of subjects are relatively rare, you may have to wait days to complete your sampling. In those cases, it is best to be practical. If you are systematically sampling by age, and only a few people in the age category "over 60" come into your institution, then you may want to include nearly all of the people in this category, regardless of when they enter. Then, when you write up your findings, consider how this might possibly have biased your results. In informal settings, there is limited control over the environment, so it is often necessary to be practical and opportunistic. You should not ignore the rules of sampling; select your sample in the most unbiased way possible, and then consider sources of bias that might necessarily result. You can choose participants in any number of ways:

- As they enter or exit the building or room
- From membership lists, visitor sign-in books, museum classes, or clubs
- From people walking near the museum or in other public places

If you want typical casual visitors for your participants, select people who are entering or leaving the building, program, or exhibit. If you are studying only people that have a more intensive involvement in the institution, use membership, class, or volunteer lists. There is never a perfect time to select participants. If you select them as they enter the institution, they may be in a hurry, concerned that they may miss time with the exhibits or programs. If you select them at the end of the visit, they may have already run out of time and need to get to their next activity. In either case, be sure to tell participants right away how much of their time you will need, and then be sure to end promptly on time. If you plan to interview adults with children, then either make the children the focus of the interview, or else provide supervised activity for the children, so the adult can focus attention on your questions. In all cases, the most important goal is to select your participants in a way that does not introduce bias.

It can be useful to offer something in exchange for your participant's time. The offer of a free pass to the facility, a free planetarium show, or a free poster or gift certificate at the museum store can be a useful way of motivating participants who might not otherwise feel inclined to give you their time. This will also help you and the participants feel more at ease because there will be less of an impression that you are imposing on their time. For longer interviews, it is best to first contact your participants at the institution or over the phone or email, and then make arrangements to meet them at a convenient time and place for the actual interview.

The time or day of the week may also impact your selection of participants because it may determine who is available to be approached. Especially if you are sampling participants from a much larger pool, be aware of the institution's pattern of use. For example, it is not unusual for school groups to visit museums on weekday mornings and for families to come during weekends. Families with young children may come mainly on weekend mornings, to avoid afternoon nap times. If you are studying family groups, you may want to sample mainly during weekend hours. If you are trying to generalize to all

Table 5.5   A plan to select participants from a pool of casual visitors.

	M	T	W	Th	F	Sa	Su
Morning							
10 a.m. to 12 noon	X		X		X		X
Afternoon							
1 p.m. to 3 p.m.		X		X		X	
Afternoon							
3 p.m. to 5 p.m.	—	—	—	—	—	—	—

types of casual visitors, however, you should select participants during all hours of active visitation. Most informal institutions (or their security personnel) can provide information on visitor-use patterns to guide your selection criteria.

Table 5.5 is an example of a plan to select participants from the pool of casual visitors to a museum that is open seven days a week from 10 a.m. to 5 p.m. In this case, the hours from 3 p.m. to 5 p.m. were avoided because participants would be tired near the end of their visit. At another museum, or in a different study, there may be good reasons for sampling during this time. This matrix can be used to assist in choosing balanced sampling times with certain times blocked out.

SELECTING PARTICIPANTS FOR QUALITATIVE STUDIES

Qualitative evaluations often require small numbers of participants that are selected for specific reasons. Typical qualitative sampling methods include the following (Patton 1987; 2008):

- *Extreme case sampling*: Choose unusual or special cases to shed light on how things work for particular individuals. Choose the "best" case or "worst" case example.
- *Maximum variation sampling*: Capture central themes and principal outcomes by selecting diverse characteristics for constructing the sample. If the program covers a broad geographical area, then select participants that represent the major features (e.g., rural, urban, and suburban). If the program reaches diverse audiences, make sure that diversity is represented in the participants.
- *Homogeneous sampling*: Pick a small sample that focuses on a particular issue of importance, for example, adults aged over 60 or children between 3 and 5 years of age.

- *Typical case sampling*: Using the help of people in the institution who know what "typical" really is, choose participants that are as close to that ideal as possible. If most of the visitors are family groups with two parents and two children, then the sample might include only these groups.
- *Critical case sampling*: Critical cases are those that are very important for some reason. For example, if your graphics can be read by visitors aged over 60, then most other age groups might be able to read them as well.
- *Chain or snowball sampling*: One subject refers you to a subject who then refers you to another, each providing their own perspective on the issue of concern.
- *Informants*: One or more people provide you with ongoing information about a situation or program. For example, a docent or volunteer may serve as an informant to convey detailed information about their training program from the perspective of a participant.

Sometimes you seek what Patton (1987) calls, "confirming cases," to include participants who might present a similar view to those already collected. For example, if physically challenged visitors in your sample encounter problems using the exhibits, then you may want to find other disabled subjects to confirm their problems. In other cases, you may want to select "contrasting cases," which you believe will differ in some interesting way from those you have already interviewed or observed. Sampling can also have political or practical motivations, for example, including a board member or an administrator as an interview subject can have the benefit of informing and reassuring them about the study. Finally, there are always occasions in which time or resources are simply limited, so you end up sampling whoever is available and taking into account possible sources of bias as you interpret the findings.

Chapter 6

Observational Tools

Observations are the most straightforward means of finding out how people use informal environments. Observations can tell you how many visitors are going to an exhibit, and how they are interacting with particular components. They can tell what group members talk about during their visit and how they respond to programs. This chapter describes four observational tools that can be employed in evaluation studies in informal environments: (1) counting, (2) tracking movements, (3) basic observations, and (4) detailed, more systematic observations. This chapter also highlights strategies for sampling visitor behaviors during observations and for recording observational data.

COUNTING PEOPLE

The most basic kind of observational study is to count the number of people. You can better understand who visits a museum by counting who comes in the door on various dates and times (Serrell 1977). You can observe the composition of visitor groups to determine whether people visit primarily as family groups or with their peers. You may want to know whether numbers of visitors differ by time of day or day of the week. A count of the number of people that visit different exhibits can indicate differences in their popularity, ease of use, or accessibility within the museum (see also Korn 1995). Counting visitors can also serve as a first step toward more in-depth studies, but it begins with the following:

- Consider how you will inform visitors that the study is occurring. Generally, a sign at the entrance informing people about the nature and reason for the evaluation project is sufficient when you are only counting numbers of people that enter the institution. If possible, let visitors know that they can request to be excluded from the count.

- Decide how you will conduct your count. You may choose to count visitors as they enter the building, but you should also investigate whether there are easier ways to gather the data. Passive methods for counting visitors, such as an automatic turnstile or cameras with counting software connected to the Internet, may already exist in the institution. Sometimes, the institution's entrance fee structure will allow you to infer visitation from each day's gate return or from the quantity of distributed tickets.
- Decide when and where you will make your counts, depending on what you want to know. Sample regularly enough so you do not bias your count with just afternoon or weekend visitors. Sometimes, it is possible for the staff at each entrance to count and categorize every person who enters.
- Construct a data collection form that specifies the observational data that you want to collect. For instance, consider the following data points: date, time, name of the person doing the counting, visitor's sex, group type (adult-child, adult only, or child only), and age category. In some cases, these records can be kept with specialized smartphone apps or dedicated devices.

TRACKING MOVEMENTS

Tracking visitor's movements within an institution or gallery can tell what exhibits or objects people choose to visit. Sometimes, the spatial arrangements of an area can encourage or discourage access to particular features. During the 1920s and 1930s, Arthur Melton (1933; 1935), Edward Robinson (Robinson 1931; Robinson, Sherman & Curry 1928), and their colleagues tracked the movements of visitors in museums, identifying several consistent patterns of spatial use. These researchers observed that all other things being equal, visitors tended to turn right when entering galleries, they tended to follow the right-hand wall, and they tended to spend less time at exhibits as they approached the exit. Very popular exhibits had paradoxical effects on the surrounding exhibits. Sometimes, they had spillover effects, encouraging visitors to use the exhibits nearby, whereas in other instances, they overshadowed surrounding exhibits, making them virtually invisible to the public. These findings have been confirmed by various researchers since that time (see Serrell 1997, for a review of this issue). Figure 6.1 shows one method of how tracking data can be displayed.

To track the movements of visitors, begin by using a simplified floor plan of the gallery or program space to trace the pattern of each visitor's

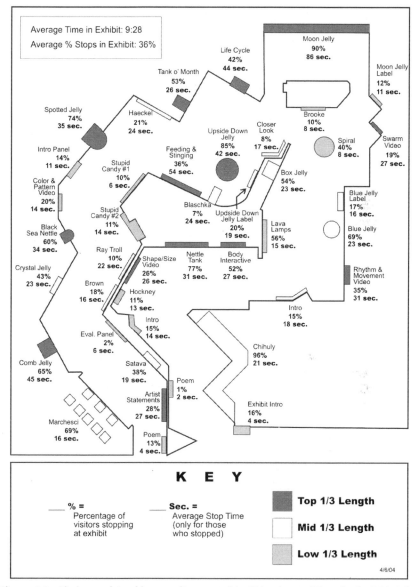

Figure 6.1 Timing and tracking results created by Yalowitz and Tomulonis (2004) for the Monterey Bay Aquarium's 4,650 square-foot Jellies: Living Art exhibit. *Source:* © Monterey Bay Aquarium.

movements. Record only one visitor's movements on a single floor plan, because an active visitor will provide a sufficiently complex pattern for interpretation. If you wish to follow family groups, then choose one member to be your focal subject, and record that person's behavior in detail, while indicating general notes on the location of the rest of the group. You may also consider asking visitors to wear devices that would track their locations as they move throughout the museum.

You may want to record time spent at various locations. Indicate those locations in advance by circling the area on your floor plan. You can fill in the circle with a time value (i.e., length of time spent at the location) as you make your recording.

You may record a code for the behavior of visitors at particular stations. Indicate those locations by drawing a square on your floor plan. Depending on the type of exhibit, you may be limited in how detailed the codes should be. The next section provides guidelines on how to code behaviors.

Collect enough tracking maps to have a good representation of the possible patterns of use of the exhibit, gallery, or institution. In many cases, that will mean collecting at least 30–50 tracking maps from a variety of visitors and over varying days and times. Then sort them into possible patterns. Use your judgment to determine what categories would be useful to sort the tracking maps. Some examples are as follows:

- *Heavy, medium, and light use*: Select typical examples that show variations in how many of the available exhibits people visit and interact with one another. Heavy use involves lots of interaction at many different exhibits. Light use may involve little time spent at the exhibits, few exhibits visited, or both.
- *Complete and incomplete visits*: Sometimes, the visitor stops at every station or exhibit, skipping few of the available opportunities for interaction. This can be considered a "complete" or thorough pattern. Contrast the most complete patterns you find with those that short-circuit the visit in various ways. Look for tracing patterns that show areas of the gallery or museum that are ignored when visitors decide to move on.
- *Fast and slow visits*: Some visitors are thorough but spend little time at any one exhibit. Contrast this pattern with those who spend a lot of time at some or all of the exhibits. Do not hesitate to create intermediate categories to show the more typical patterns.
- *Intensive, focused, and minimal use*: Intensive use might refer to a long time spent at relatively few exhibits. Focused use might refer to a moderate time spent at few exhibits. Minimal use might refer to a short time at few exhibits.

BASIC OBSERVATIONS

Basic observations can be as simple as including behavioral information in tracking visitors' movements. Include information on behaviors that give information that is most important to you, but be sure to make the codes descriptive of observable behaviors. For example, you may not be able to verify whether a visitor read the exhibit label, unless she or he read it aloud. Therefore, you might want to use the categories, "look at label" and "read label aloud." If there was no time to make a notation about behavior, then leave the box blank. Some behaviors and possible codes to use when making brief observations include the following:

le	look at exhibit only
man	manipulate exhibit
ce	comment, exhibit related
cn	comment, not exhibit related
qe	question, exhibit related
lat	look at label/graphic
ra	read label aloud
nn	none of the above

Basic observations can go beyond counting people and tracking movements. They are designed to describe and measure specific behaviors in people's everyday lives. An advantage of such observations is that they allow the evaluator to better understand the situation or context being studied. They provide direct information about what visitors are actually doing in an institution or a program, and they offer opportunities for identifying unanticipated outcomes.

Basic observations can be useful during front-end, formative, and summative phases of evaluation. During the front-end phase, basic observations can provide a background context for how visitors interact before changes are made. During the formative phase, this data collection tool can provide feedback on program and exhibit implementation and delivery mechanisms. Basic observations are also useful during summative evaluation as a way of assessing the degree to which visitors engage with various exhibits and with each other throughout their experience.

When used in formative evaluation, basic observation can help to improve a program while it is still in operation. For instance, evaluators observed urban teenagers in an after-school program designed to increase their interest in and knowledge of astronomy (Foutz & Koke 2007). Because the staff was trying to achieve a relaxed, collaborative atmosphere for learning, the researchers focused on the interaction between program facilitators and teens and on how program spaces were set up. Observation data showed that the programs were more structured than the staff had intended, and that spaces were set up in a didactic, lecture-style fashion. As a result of these observations, the program staff added more small-group discussion to the program, so that teens had more opportunities for collaboration.

To make basic observations, there are several steps involved. First, consider what role the evaluator will play during data collection. Observational strategies differ depending on whether the evaluator is a participant in the setting being studied. Typically, a distinction is made between the evaluator as an onlooker and the evaluator as a participant. As an onlooker, the evaluator basically tries to remain inconspicuous, exerting minimal influence on the participants' actions. As a participant, the evaluator uses his or her presence as an advantage in collecting information, fully integrating into the experience being observed. According to Patton,

> The ideal is to negotiate and adopt that degree of participation that will yield the most meaningful data about the program given the characteristics of the participants, the nature of the staff-participant interactions, and the sociopolitical context of the program. [Patton 1990, p. 209]

Participant observation originated from the tradition of anthropologists and sociologists who were studying other cultures and immersing themselves into the experience of those cultures, sometimes for as long as several years. In program evaluation, participant observation can involve relatively short exposures with various levels of involvement. In an evaluation of a docent or volunteer program, the evaluator may choose to undergo training and begin to perform volunteer activities, effectively becoming a member of the volunteer group. Similarly, the evaluator may choose to enroll in a class or experience a program with family or friends. The key to participant evaluation is immersion, so that the evaluator can feel what it is like to be a member of the group being studied.

Because of age, sex, background, or ethnicity, the evaluator may not always have the option for full participation in an activity. This can sometimes be rectified when the evaluator includes individuals that belong to the groups being studied as members of the research team. Some situations, however, will not afford that opportunity. Patton (1987, p. 76) describes the following exchange between a prisoner and a young evaluator who was doing participant observation in a prison:

Inmate: "What you here for, man?"

Evaluator: "I'm here for a while to find out what's it like to be in prison."

I: "What do you mean—'find out what it's like'?"

E: "I'm here so I can experience prison from the inside instead of just studying what it's like from out there."

I: "You got to be jerkin' me off, man. Experience from the inside? Shit, man. You can go home when you decide you've had enough can't you?"

E: "Yeah."

I: "Then you ain't never gonna know what it's like from the inside."

In addition to deciding whether to be a participant, the evaluator must also decide how to portray the purpose of the observations to participants. Wherever possible, it is best to be straightforward with visitors about what you are doing, and why you are doing it, as outlined in Chapter 4 on research ethics. When conducting observations at an institution or exhibition, clear signage at the outset of the experience can help visitors to know that there is the possibility that they may be observed during their experience and how those observations will be used. When conducting program observations, an announcement at the outset of the program lets participants know who the observer is and what role they are playing throughout the program.

Determining the scope or focus is also a critical step in conducting basic observations. It is not possible to observe everything. Consider what you will specifically look for and what you will *not* pay attention to. Patton (1990) distinguishes between a broad focus for observations, encompassing almost all aspects of the setting, and a narrow focus, involving only a small component or piece of what is happening. Decisions about focus are typically informed by the evaluation design and the nature of the questions being asked. For instance, you may be most interested in knowing how visitors interact with a specific component within a gallery or how visitors interact with one another.

Another consideration is how to decide who you will observe. Often, it is useful to select a representative sample, one that mirrors the overall population who use an exhibition or participate in a program. In this way, it is more likely that your basic observations will hold true for a larger audience. Other times, when the purpose of the basic observations is formative, you may want to be more opportunistic, seeking out participants who represent defined subgroups of users.

Once you have decided who your study participants are, consider how you will record data from your basic observations. Typically, these observations are guided by some form of structured protocol. The protocol can take various forms, ranging from a detailed narrative in the form of field notes to a checklist or rating scale of specific behaviors that address the evaluation questions of interest. Using a protocol increases the likelihood that all observers are

Table 6.1 Engagement scale developed by Falk & Holland (1991) to assess visitors' engagement with exhibits.

1. Minimal/Glance	Visitor stops, pauses briefly, and glances at one or more elements, but demonstrates no apparent interest in any particular element or information.
2. Cursory	Visitor stops, watches/views elements briefly in a cursory way, perhaps casually points to something, and glances at text panels, but demonstrates no apparent interaction with the interactive.
3. Moderate	Visitor stops, views several elements of the interactive with apparent interest, reads some text, and appears somewhat engaged and focused.
4. Extensive	Visitor stops, views most elements of the interactive very intently; reads some text and appears very engaged and focused.

gathering relevant data and, with appropriate training, applying the same criteria in their observations. For detailed narratives and field notes, Patton (1990, p. 273) offers the following guidelines:

- Be as descriptive as possible.
- Gather a variety of information from different perspectives.
- Triangulate by gathering different kinds of data. For example, you can compare observational data with interviews conducted with participants, or with program documentation or photographs.
- Use quotations. Represent program participants in their own terms. Capture participants' views of their experiences in their own words.
- Experience the program or exhibit as fully as possible, while maintaining an analytical perspective.
- Clearly separate description from interpretation and judgment.
- Include in your field notes your own experiences, thoughts, and feelings. These are also field data.

Simple categories or rating scales can also be useful ways of recording basic observations. A simple engagement scale (Table 6.1) can record the extent to which visitors' engage with an interactive exhibit component, and it can focus observations by articulating categories at the outset, as opposed to coding narrative field notes after the fact.

DETAILED OBSERVATIONS

Detailed observations provide information about *what* visitors actually do in informal educational environments. This method has been used by numerous researchers to understand how informal learning occurs, to understand sex and age differences in out-of-school learning, and perhaps most importantly, to observe how social interactions contribute to the informal learning experience.

Detailed observations have been conducted in museums and other informal educational environments since the studies of Edward Robinson and Arthur Melton in the 1920s and 1930s. Over the years, researchers have conducted observations while following visitors on foot or causally joining their groups (e.g., Diamond 1980; McManus 1987), and they have observed them using footage from security video cameras (Falk 1983). These findings have had a major impact on how educators view the experience of visiting a museum, zoo, aquarium, or park. Two decades of observational studies in these settings have created an awareness of the central importance of visitors' social interactions in informal learning. These studies have shown that social experience is often a primary motivation for the visits and that social interaction is a fundamental part of the teaching and learning (Crowley et al. 2001; Davis et al. 2015; Falk & Dierking 1992).

Conducting detailed observations requires decisions about which recording equipment, which observational categories, and what behavioral sampling technique to use. More information about recording detailed behavior can be found in Martin & Bateson (2007) and Yoder & Symons (2010).

A first step in conducting detailed observations can be to create an ethogram. The word *ethogram* was popularized by Konrad Lorenz, a Nobel Prize-winning biologist. It refers to the sum total of an animal's behavioral repertoire and is used widely by biologists who record the behavior of wild animals in their natural habitat (Lorenz 1950). An ethogram is a list of the major categories of behaviors that a species displays. Conducting observations of visitors in a museum or zoo has many similarities to observing wild animals in nature. In both settings, the observer tries to record the natural behavior of the subject with minimal influence by the researcher. A museum or zoo ethogram is a list of the behavioral categories that visitors display while in those settings.

Diamond (1982) suggests that a first step in constructing an ethogram is to conduct a series of preliminary observations during which you make a list of all of the behaviors that you see your visitors display. You can add other behaviors that you observed previously, even if they do not occur in the preliminary sessions. You may choose to begin with lists of behaviors that have been published by other researchers, then modify them by observing the particular audience you plan to study.

The second step to ethogram construction is to define each behavior explicitly, so it focuses on specific actions rather than on interpretations or judgments. Behaviors should be described on the basis of observable features; do not include behaviors that require you to guess what the visitor is feeling. We mentioned previously that you cannot tell if a subject is reading the exhibit labels, unless he or she reads aloud. Instead, use two categories: "look at label" and "read label aloud." Similarly, you can observe a visitor smiling, but you cannot observe whether he or she is "happy." Therefore, "smile" is the more appropriate category.

You will need to be aware of whether your behavioral categories are events or states. Some kinds of analysis will require you to use only one or the other. *Events* are behavioral patterns of relatively short duration, such as "touch," "ask question," "hit," or "read aloud." *States* are behavioral patterns of generally long duration, such as "rest," "wait," and "sit."

Decide whether you will measure latency, frequency, duration, or intensity:

- Latency is the time it takes before the first occurrence of a behavior. Latency can be timed from a variable in the environment, or it can be signaled by the visitor's own actions (e.g., the time from when a visitor approaches an exhibit to when she or he starts to use it).
- *Frequency* is the number of occurrences of a behavior per unit time. For example, it can refer to how many times a family member engages in manipulate exhibit or how often a child asks questions during a program.
- *Duration* is the length of time of a single occurrence of the behavioral pattern. For example, it can be how long visitors continue to interact with an exhibit or how long they spend looking at the graphics.
- *Intensity* is a graded measure of behavior. For example, movement could be rated "run," "fast walk," or "slow walk," and the frequency of each speed category is recorded.

Specify the time period that your observations will last. For example, it could be from when the visitor first approaches the exhibit to when he or she leaves, or it could be from the time a family group enters to when they leave the institution. Finally, code your behavioral categories in a way that is easy for you to remember. It is usually easier to remember categories that are abbreviated in two to three letter codes ("lat" for look at; "man" for manipulate exhibit) than categories that are given numerical designations.

Typically, ethograms involve long lists of behavioral categories. An ethogram of 70 categories was used by Judy Diamond (1980; 1986) in her study of family groups at the Exploratorium and the Lawrence Hall of Science. Each category is defined in terms of observable behaviors. Sometimes, however, it is more practical to use shorter lists of behaviors. The list of behavioral codes is the vocabulary of behavioral observations. Just as you might construct sentences from word lists, observers construct behavioral descriptions from the list of behavioral categories. The exact record of what the visitor is observed to do is recorded as "sentences" made up of the category codes or columns of single categories. Most often, when the notes are taken by hand, the behavioral categories are abbreviated with one or two letter codes, so that they can be recorded quickly.

BEHAVIORAL SAMPLING

An important step in conducting detailed observations is to choose your behavioral sampling method. Because the behaviors of a visitor unfold in a continuous stream of information and activity, the observer needs to decide how to select, or sample, from the continuous flow. The most commonly used method of sampling behavior is called *focal individual sampling*. In this method, the observer chooses a single individual and observes his or her behavior for the duration of the session. When the focal visitor is out of sight, the observations are stopped until he or she returns.

Observations of social behaviors can be made with focal individual sampling by noting all the interactions a visitor has with other people. When observing family groups, you can choose to observe one person per group whose characteristics are decided in advance (e.g., adult female or oldest child). If you are fairly sure, however, that two people will stay together, you can use focal dyad sampling, in which you record the behavior of a pair of visitors, such as a parent and child.

When using focal individual sampling, the observer typically records a continuous stream of behaviors in an attempt to make the most complete record possible. This is called *continuous recording*. Beginning and end times are usually specified in advance. For example, the first approach of a child to an exhibit could signal the beginning of a continuous recording session, and his or her exit from the exhibit could signal the end. This type of recording is feasible when making a video record of an event, and then replaying that record for detailed, or sometimes even frame-by-frame, analysis. An audio record of behavior can work the same way; you can speak a continuous description of behavioral events into a tape recorder for later transcription. Continuous recording is also possible on a laptop, where the program automatically keeps track of time. In formative evaluation, it is possible to do a rough version of continuous recording by exposing a visitor to an exhibit and then using codes to record a continuous description of what the visitor does. Although the recording may not be in great detail, it may accurately represent how the subject used the exhibit, and this information can be a valuable source of information for exhibit designers.

With focal individual sampling, it is also possible to select a unit of time and then record what behaviors are occurring at the end of each interval.

This is called *time sampling*. For example, you might note at 3-minute intervals whether the subject is active or resting. Recording this data throughout the course of the visit might help you determine where resting stations should be located. For time sampling, the behaviors are usually noted ahead of time on a check sheet, and at each interval, time is entered next to the appropriate behavior. In a variation on this technique, called *one-zero sampling*, the observer notes the presence or absence of a behavior at regular intervals. This sampling is most useful when the sampling interval is relatively frequent, such as each minute.

Individual sampling may not be the best choice when a lot of data on individual visitors are not needed. An alternative technique, *scan sampling*, records the behavior of all members of an entire group at regular intervals. For example, every 30 minutes, you could note what each individual in a single museum gallery is doing. Over the course of the day, this sample would provide a rough measure of visitor behavior in that gallery. Because scan sampling has to occur quickly, it is often biased toward highly visible behaviors, and thus may not provide an accurate representation of what individual visitors do.

Another method of selecting what to observe is called *behavior sampling*. In this technique, the observer watches a group of visitors and then records each occurrence of a particular behavior. The observer usually also notes something about the context for that behavior, who was involved, or at which exhibit it occurred. For example, an observer may stand at one exhibit and record the length of time that each visitor spends looking at the labels. This may give a rough idea of how much attention is given to the label and by whom. Behavior sampling is usually used to study relatively infrequent behaviors.

When making preliminary observations to generate the behavior categories, an observer may use *ad lib sampling*. In this sampling method, the observer records whatever is visible and interesting at any time, there is no set schedule for making the observations. The method may also be used during participant observation, when the observer may be a part of the activity being observed. In this case, the observer takes notes, as he or she is able. Sometimes, ad lib sampling is also useful during an uncommon or unpredictable event, such as the appearance of a famous or entertaining person, an unusually large crowd, or an emergency, such as an earthquake.

Chapter 7

Interviews and Questionnaires

Interviews and questionnaires provide insight into visitors' thoughts, ideas, and opinions from their own personal perspective. In this chapter, we explore both interviews and questionnaires as tools for understanding visitors and their experiences.

INTERVIEW GUIDELINES

If conducted in a responsible manner, interviews can be valuable tools for assessing visitors' thoughts and experiences. Interviews can yield rich, detailed data. They permit personal contact with respondents, allowing the interviewer to explain or clarify questions, and they provide opportunities for in-depth exploration of topics.

How interview questions are asked has a profound influence on the quality of information received. The goal of a well-conducted interview is to elicit a participant's responses in ways that avoid the imposition of bias on the part of the interviewer. A bias-free interview is one in which the participant feels comfortable and safe, where there is no implied judgment or criticism by the interviewer, and where the participant feels unhampered in answering the questions in an open and honest manner. The creation of interview and survey questions requires careful design. Useful guides that can help evaluators design their questions can be found in Tourangeau, Rips, & Rasinski (2000) and Sudman, Bradburn, & Schwarz (1996).

Interviews can involve one participant at a time, or they can involve groups of participants. Interviews can be as casual as a conversation or as formal as a list of questions prepared in advance and asked in exactly the same way for each participant. The nature of the interview, however, determines how the findings can be analyzed and constrains the interpretation of the data. Quantitative interviews are relatively formal and structured, and the responses can be analyzed statistically. Qualitative interviews, on the other hand, rely more on conversation to probe deeply and explore interesting new directions. The results are usually presented in narrative form, summarizing major trends or alternatives. Here are some general guidelines that apply to all kinds of interviews:

- Plan in advance how you will locate and choose your participants. Arrange times and locations with participants ahead of time for interviews that last more than 15 or 20 minutes.
- Be honest and open with the participants. Tell them the purpose of the interview and ask permission to include them in the study. A tone of openness and honesty is not only ethically appropriate, but it also will make participants feel comfortable about responding in an open and honest manner.
- Find a place and time for the interview that will be comfortable and convenient for participants. Try to arrange for an interview location that provides privacy. If participants with families are included, provide supervised activities for children, so they will not distract. If young children are the focus of the interview, include a means for caregivers to participate.
- Ask only those questions that are necessary for your study. Any question, no matter how innocuous, is an intrusion into the privacy of the participant. Do not ask things unless you are sure you require the answers. Have good reasons for asking questions, especially personal ones. The evaluation design should guide what questions really need to be asked.
- When you arrange your questions, order them so the most personal questions come last. Participants differ in what they consider personal, but people can be sensitive about revealing their age, income, how long they have lived in the country, and sometimes even their name and address. If you require this information for a study, ask it at the end of the interview. This gives the participants a chance to get to know you before they are expected to give information that relates most closely to them. Occasionally, participants react to sensitive questions by refusing to participate further in the interview.
- It is sometimes easier for participants to place themselves in a category that gives a range of ages or incomes, rather than a specific value. For example, instead of asking a participant's age, provide categories that include various age ranges, and ask your participants to indicate the appropriate one. Instead of asking for the participant's annual household income, you could ask, "In which of the following categories does your household income belong? Under $30,000; $30,001 to $60,000; $60,001 to $90,000; over $90,000?"

- Ask only one item at a time. If you wish to ask about a person's strengths and weaknesses, first ask about strengths, and then in a separate question, ask about weaknesses. Do not expect the participant to remember several questions phrased as one.
- Pilot test your interview questions first. Such testing will tell you which questions are confusing, and where participants may interpret questions differently than you intended.

Patton emphasizes that it is the responsibility of the interviewer to make it clear to the participant what is being asked. This requires asking well-phrased questions in a language that the participants will understand:

> In preparing to do an interview, first find out how the people you are interviewing commonly talk about the program being studied. Use language that is understandable and part of the frame of reference of the person being interviewed. During the interview pay attention to what language the respondent uses to describe the setting, program participants, special activities, or whatever else is reported. The interviewer then uses the language provided by the interviewee in the rest of the interview. Questions that use the respondent's own languages are those that are most likely to be clear. (Patton 1987, p. 23)

INFORMAL CONVERSATIONAL INTERVIEWS

Different kinds of interviews bring with them advantages and limitations. One of the most common kinds of interviews is the informal conversational interview or unstructured interview. This is an open-ended approach to interviewing, typical of many qualitative studies. The interviewer allows the nature of the conversation to direct the questioning. After the first exchanges with the participant, the questions emerge from the course of the discussion. When an important or interesting idea is raised, it may be pursued with follow-up or more in-depth questioning.

The conversational mode is probably the least threatening way of conducting interviews. It can be a valuable tool for probing a participant's feelings. At the time of the interview, participants often have not had time to consider their feelings about an exhibit or a program, and when they are confronted by an interviewer who asks their opinion, they may find that they really do not have one. In a conversational interview, however, participants are able to think about, probe, discuss, and sometimes even test their ideas. They can gain clarity in their own beliefs, and this can provide useful insights. In addition, this open-ended interviewing approach allows the evaluator to be highly responsive to individual differences and the surrounding context.

Informal conversation interviews also have disadvantages. Some participants are highly suggestible, and they may quickly incorporate their ideas of
what they think the interviewer wants into their own belief system. These
participants may report on what they believe the interviewer wants to hear,
instead of their own thoughts, beliefs, or experiences. Other participants may
not have a fixed belief or opinion and frequently change their ideas throughout
the conversational interview. Also, data gathered through informal conversational interviews can be challenging to analyze because different questions
have been asked of different people, resulting in different responses. Despite
these disadvantages, the informal conversational interview can be a valuable
source of ideas and general impressions.

SEMI-STRUCTURED INTERVIEWS

Another kind of interview is called the *semi-structured interview*. In this
method, the interviewer specifies topics and issues for the interview but
leaves open the exact way that questions will be asked. You may identify a
series of topics that need to be covered, but how each question is asked may
depend on the circumstances of the particular interview. The semi-structured interview is particularly useful when interviewing children. It may
be important to know that the same topics are covered with each child,
but not all of the subjects may understand the same words, either because
their language abilities are not well developed or because English is not
their primary language. This interview technique allows the researcher to
substitute words that may be more easily understood or sometimes to ask
a question in several different ways. It is useful to plan out a list of topics
and general question areas in advance, along with cues for areas to probe
for more detail
   One form of semi-structured interview is the focus group. Focus groups
are composed of participants who are similar in some specific way, either
because of their interests, past experience, or membership in a particular
demographic or social category. Focus groups are often used to learn how a
target audience might react to a specific product or planned program. They
capitalize on group dynamics, using group interaction to generate data that
would be unlikely to emerge in an individual interview. The disadvantage of
focus groups is that individuals may not be willing to voice opinions that are
not shared by other members of the group.
   Another source of usual information can come from an expert panel, a
group of people who have particular expertise related to an exhibit or a
program and are invited together for sharing this experience or knowledge

(Fischer 1997). For instance, in a study in an art museum, Andrews (1979) invited a dozen high school students to serve on an expert panel. The teenagers helped the researchers to interpret data from a questionnaire that had been sent to 520 young adults. The researchers also asked the students about their best and worst experiences with museums, the relationship between school and the museum, their attitudes about the value of museum visits, and their reactions to unfamiliar art. The teenage experts talked frankly to the researchers about young people's educational priorities and special interests. In this way, a panel of experts not only provided information for the evaluation, but they also assisted in the data interpretation.

STRUCTURED INTERVIEWS

Of all the interview types, structured interviews lend themselves best to statistical analysis. In interviews of this type, the questions and response categories are previously determined and tested ahead of time, enabling the findings from large samples of participants to be summarized and analyzed. As is the case for all interview types, the form of the questions in a structured interview will greatly influence how a participant responds. As previously mentioned, participants often find it easier to place their opinions in a category, rather than provide a direct answer. If categorical alternatives are given in an interview, provide them in writing on a card so that the participants do not have to memorize them. This standardized approach to interviewing minimizes interviewer effects, because the same question is asked of each participant in exactly the same way. It also streamlines data analysis. However, structured interviews do not permit the evaluator to pursue unanticipated topics or to individualize the questions based on the visitor's responses. When clarification to a question is needed, researchers typically have scripted prompts that they will use with all participants (*Can you tell me more about that?*) to provide a uniform experience.

One comprehensive interview project was initiated by a group of Bay Area museums in order to improve their understanding of multicultural constituencies (Museum Management Consultants, Inc. & Polaris Research and Development 1994). The authors interviewed a sample of 1,697 adult residents in the San Francisco Bay Area, selecting participants from random telephone lists that were purchased for each of three nonwhite ethnic groups in the region. It required a total of 15,313 calls to get an acceptable number of respondents.

The researchers had specific criteria for whom to include (e.g., individuals had to be adults aged over 17, and they had to have visited a museum at least once in their life). The interview protocol was first tested in advance with a small number of participants. Then respondents were interviewed over the phone by trained bilingual interviewers who offered to conduct the interviews in English, Spanish, Cantonese, Mandarin, or Tagalog. The interviews included closed and open-ended questions, as well as questions about the respondents' demographic characteristics. For example, in the following closed question, the interviewers read both the question and the possible answers to the respondent:

Who would you usually go with on a trip to a museum? Would it be . . . ?

1. With a friend
2. With your family
3. With your spouse or partner
4. By yourself
5. With a group

Other questions were asked as open-ended questions, and then the interviewer immediately categorized the responses. In the following example, the answers were not read aloud to the participant:

What kinds of things would encourage you to go to a museum more often?
   (Possible answers; not read aloud)

1. Better transportation
2. More exhibits based on your culture
3. Lower entrance fee
4. Available day care
5. More activities for your family
6. Different hours
7. Nothing
8. Free day
9. Something else _____
10. Don't know
11. Refused

Other questions were completely open ended:

When you think of "museums," what is the first thing that comes to mind?

Still other questions included rating scales:

I'm going to read you a list of visitor services or amenities that are found in museums. Please tell me whether the visitor service is very important (4), important (3), somewhat important (2), or not important to you (1)?

a. People who can answer your questions	1	2	3	4
b. Information about what is there and how to get around	1	2	3	4
c. Visitor maps and signs	1	2	3	4
d. Information in languages other than English	1	2	3	4

The final questions, which were necessary for the study, were also the most personal and intrusive:

Which country were you born in? How long have you lived in this country? Which country were your parents born in?

Through the use of a wide range of question types, a carefully designed selection procedure, and experienced interviewers, the authors gained a comprehensive picture of how multicultural audiences experience museums. This type of study can provide the museums of an entire region with information that can help them diversify and expand their audiences.

ASKING QUESTIONS

The quality of an interview depends largely on how the questions are asked. Questions should be free from bias, allowing participants to answer based on their personal opinions. For instance, asking a participant "What did you like about the exhibit?" assumes that there was something they liked. Asking participants "Did you visit the museum today to spend time together as a family?" presupposes the answer. The challenge in writing interview questions is to ensure that visitors will understand what you are asking and give you information without your direct influence.

To phrase good questions, it is useful to consider what the participant would need to do to answer your question. Answering what may seem to be easy questions can be surprisingly difficult, requiring much more time than the evaluator might at first expect. Consider what would seem to be a straightforward question: How many times have you visited a museum in the past year? It turns out that this simple question is not so simple to answer. First, the participant needs to think about a relatively rare event (visiting a museum) among thousands of different events that might occur in a year. Answering this question accurately may be difficult, and even if the participant can come up with an answer, it might take considerable time. Moreover, different participants may define both "museum" and "visit" differently. Does a brief trip to a small collection count? Do multiple visits to the same museum count? And how does the participant define "past year"—is it the calendar year or the past twelve months? Seemingly simple questions are often not so easy.

Moreover, the way in which a question is asked, or the way in which participants are asked to provide an answer can dramatically affect how they interpret a question. For example, suppose that in the previous question regarding the number of visits to a museum we asked participants to use a scale to provide an answer, rather than simply giving a number. Suppose that the scale were as follows: None, 1–3, 4–6, 7–9, or 10 or more times.

The presence of the scale provides a great deal of information, even though neither the participant nor the interviewer may realize that information is being communicated. For example, the presence of a tick box for "10 or more times" communicates that some visitors go to the museum quite often. Such knowledge can alter how people search their own memory; the presence of particular categories of responses can serve as cognitive anchors that bias people's memory for events. In the preceding example, the presence of a category of 10 or more times may lead participants to say that they visit museums more often than if they were simply asked to give a single estimate.

Probing or follow-up questions can deepen the initial response given by the participant, especially in informal conversational interviews and semi-structured interviews. Detail-oriented probes focus on the basic who, where, what, when, and how of the situation to gather more detail (i.e., When did that happen? Who else was involved? Why did you do that?). Elaboration probes encourage the participant to continue talking; these include simple things such as head nodding or a confirmation that you are listening (i.e., Uh-huh). Elaboration probes also include questions such as "Could you say more?" and "That's helpful. Can you give more detail?"

In a long open or semi-structured interview, it can be useful to recapitulate what you understand has been said. Recapitulation aids your understanding of the speaker's perspective while you are with the participant, and it can serve as a reliability check. Often, it will stimulate the speaker to embellish or clarify the original statement. You can begin a recapitulation with one of the following phrases: *I want to be sure I understand what you are saying* . . . OR . . . *Let me see if I understand what you are telling me* . . .

Sometimes, participants find it difficult to respond to direct questions in an interview. It may be easier for them to answer hypothetical questions about what someone else might think or to describe in a picture what a person might feel. These techniques allow participant literally to *project* their feelings and thoughts onto an imagined situation, picture, or inanimate object.

For example, instead of asking a participant what was difficult for him or her, you can ask, "What do you think other visitors would find difficult?" "How would you describe the exhibit to one of your friends?" This can increase a participant's comfort level by putting a little distance between the person and their response. Similarly, informal researchers have used drawings or photographs to help the visitor to imagine the situation that they are asked to discuss. Rosenfeld (1982) refers to these as "picture-stimulus questions" (Figure 7.1).

Figure 7.1   Images used for picture-stimulus questions created by Rosenfeld (1982) for an experimental mini-zoo at the Lawrence Hall of Science.

Personal meaning mapping (PMM) is another useful strategy for asking interview questions (Storksdieck & Falk 2005). PMM is based on concept mapping, a technique developed by Novak (1977) as a means of representing students' emerging scientific knowledge. Storksdieck and Falk adapted this technique to measure conceptual change in an informal learning environment. In application, individuals are given a piece of paper with a cueing word, phrase, or image in the center (i.e., living things) and asked to write down as many words or thoughts as come to mind related to the cue. An individual's responses form the basis for an open-ended interview in which the individual is asked to explain why they wrote what they did and to expand on their thoughts and ideas relative to the cue. These verbal responses are then recorded. Where PMM is used to measure attitudinal change, the individual goes through this process both prior and subsequent to an educational intervention, and responses are compared along four coding dimensions including extent, breadth, depth, and mastery.

This approach uses an individual's perceptions, ideas, and language as the starting point for an interview. Qualitative responses are then coded into distinct categories, and the data are analyzed quantitatively. In a summative study of the *Bone Zone* exhibit at The Children's Museum of Indianapolis, Indiana, evaluators used PMMs to better understand how visitors' exhibit experience contributed to their thinking about the biology and culture of bones (Luke et al. 2002). Upon entering the exhibit, visitors were asked to respond to the single prompt "bones." Upon exiting, these same visitors were asked to add to, subtract from, or otherwise modify what they had initially shared. Pre-exhibit and post-exhibit responses were compared, and results showed that after their exhibit experience, visitors had a greater range of vocabulary with which to discuss the topic and were more likely to associate bones with nutrition, one of the key principles of the exhibit.

Acklie (2003) used a similar projective technique, called *relationship maps*, to measure impacts of role models in the *Wonderwise Women in Science* kits. In this program, middle school-aged kids view video of a female scientist and then engage in activities related to her research (Diamond et al. 1996; Spiegel et al. 2005). Acklie gave each subject a paper with a small circle in the center, and asked the kids to place themselves at the center of the map like the sun. Then they were asked to place on the map the names of people who were important in their lives: individuals who were most important were placed closer to the center of the map; those less influential were placed further out. Youth were asked to place a star next to the individual on their map they would most wanted to be like. Finally, subjects were given a sticker with the face of the Wonderwise scientist on it, asked to place it on their map, and then explain why it was placed in that position. Interviewers then interviewed the subjects about the maps. Analysis of the maps illustrated the different levels of relationship that youth had formed with the scientist in the series.

QUESTIONNAIRE GUIDELINES

When you ask a participant to respond to written questions on paper or computer, this is usually referred to as a questionnaire or survey. Questionnaires sometimes have advantages over interviews because they can be given out to participants without the evaluator being present, and the evaluator may be less likely to have an influence on participants' responses. However, questionnaires have the disadvantage that there is no way to clarify participants' answers, and there is often no way to validate the accuracy of the responses.

To ensure that the questions posed on a questionnaire are clearly understood, they should be pilot tested beforehand. In presenting a draft of your questionnaire to a small sample of participants, you can either ask them to reflect on their interpretation of the questions or review their responses to see if the answers appear unambiguous. Record how long it takes for the participants to fill out the questionnaire, so you can determine whether it is of a reasonable length. It may also be useful to first ask the questionnaire items in an interview, where you can ask the participants to restate their answers to clarify their intentions. Results from the practice sessions can then be used to rephrase questions to be more effective.

As is the case with interviews, how the language in a questionnaire is phrased will influence the responses of the participants. According to Roger Miles and his colleagues,

> The actual words used in a questionnaire are so obviously crucial that it is surprising how often they tend to be phrased in a technical language or assume a particular class-bound mode of expression. Question wording should be free from technical terms (unless, of course, it is written for technical people), unambiguous and to the point. Furthermore, questions should be written in a language that is acceptable and appropriate to the visitors being interviewed, but this does not mean visitors should be talked down to. The fundamental precept in writing questionnaires is to imagine the people who are going to be asked to answer, and develop questions that are understandable and appropriate to them. (Miles, et al. 1988, p. 161)

At the beginning of the questionnaire, briefly tell the purpose of the study and the institutional sponsor. Written informed consent is usually required, and special considerations for consent may be required if the questionnaire participants are children, the disabled, or any other population that is at risk (see Chapter 4). If a questionnaire is mailed to respondents, always include a letter of introduction.

Try to minimize the amount of time it takes for someone to fill out the questionnaire. Generally, the longer it takes to fill out the questionnaire, the fewer people will choose to respond. Try to make the process of filling out the questionnaire an enjoyable experience. It should not feel like taking a test.

After all, you are asking the participant to give you something valuable—their time and information. An enjoyable or fun survey can be a reward in itself. For children, making a questionnaire fun can be as simple as including happy and sad faces as options to express their feelings, using a bright colored paper, or placing appropriate little figures in the margins, although it should not be so cluttered that it impairs one's ability to read or respond. You can also consider more tangible rewards for participating in your study. A free admission ticket, a poster, a logo pin or pencil, or a reduced rate on a membership can make participants feel positive about having given their time.

One of the most common types of questionnaires used in a museum is the demographic survey (see also Hooper-Greenhill 1994; Hood & Roberts 1994). These typically ask about the audience's sex, age of children, experience with the institution (e.g., number of times visited), educational background, and interests as they relate to the institution being studied. Demographic surveys should not request personal information such as participants' income, where they live, or their religious or political affiliation, unless it is imperative for the study. In general, demographic surveys are most accurate when they request factual information about a participant's background or opinions on a topic, and they are least accurate when they request detailed quantitative information (e.g., For how long did you visit the zoo today? or How many exhibits did you visit?). Participants may have clear ideas about who they are and what they feel, but they are often poor estimators of time and specific quantities.

Questions commonly asked in demographic surveys conducted in informal educational environments include the following:

How many times have you visited before?
How many times have you visited in the past 12 months?
When did you first plan your visit?
Why did you visit today?
How did you learn about (the institution or program)?
How long did you plan to stay for your visit?
Did you have plans to see any particular exhibit or event?
What did you expect to do or see during your visit?
What exhibits did you remember having visited?
What do you remember about the visit that interested you most?
How far do you live from (the institution)?
Where did you park?
Who did you visit with?
What do you do for a living?
What is your educational background?
Do you have a background in the subject matter of this institution?

To which age group do you belong?
To which gender group do you belong?

Sometimes, the order in which the responses are presented can influence the participant's choice. Salant and Dillman (1994) suggest that oftentimes participants tend to pick the first answer when filling out a paper-and-pencil questionnaire that they received in the mail. On the other hand, in telephone or face-to-face interviews, they tend to pick the last. If you think that respondents are choosing the first answer they are presented with, then it might be useful to vary the order of the responses. If your choices are, for example, "more," "about the same," or "less," then have a third of the questionnaires each use a different first answer.

Whenever possible, phrase your questions to make it as easy as possible for someone to respond. Sometimes it is more trouble to answer a question that is very general. For example, instead of asking, "How much would you spend for your museum visit?" you might ask the question as follows:

About how much money would you spend on the following?

Planetarium show	$_____
Educational program	$_____
IMAX theater presentation	$_____
Use of interactive kit	$_____
Entry into discovery room	$_____
General admission	$_____

Make the questionnaire as easy as possible to return. If you expect participants to fill out the questionnaire in the museum, then provide a comfortable location for them to answer the questions. Survey responses can be collected over the web or via social media through the use of tools like Survey Monkey or Qualtrics.

As is the case with interviews, if you have to ask personal questions, include them at the end of the questionnaire. Ask the participants whether they would like to see a report on the findings, and leave space for them to give their name and address so you can reply to them. Be sure to express your gratitude to participants for giving you their time.

WRITING QUESTIONS

Questionnaires, like interviews, can be qualitative or quantitative. A qualitative approach to a questionnaire is open ended: the participants can respond to the questions in their own manner, generating their own ideas in their own words. Participants may be asked to generate their own questions, or they may be given the opportunity to respond by drawing pictures. One question-naire contained one item on a mostly blank, but brightly colored page: "What do you want to tell us about our library?" Often, adult participants will prefer to type answers on a computer rather than writing responses by hand, but typing is not effective for younger children.

Quantitative approaches to questionnaires tend to be more structured. The questions may include various choices for answers, so that the responses can be categorized effectively. Some questions on questionnaires are best asked by providing various rating options. For more detailed discussion on rating questions, consult DeVellis (2003).

Some questionnaires will include a rating scale listing numbers from one to three or one to five, with each number symbolizing a value:

What were you interested in during high school? (Circle your response to each)

	Not at all		Some		Very Much
People or friends	1	2	3	4	5
Sports	1	2	3	4	5
Science or math or technology	1	2	3	4	5
Politics or social issues	1	2	3	4	5
Art or music or theater	1	2	3	4	5
Reading or literature	1	2	3	4	5
Other_____	1	2	3	4	5

To what extent do you agree or disagree with the statement: _____?

1. Strongly disagree
2. Somewhat disagree
3. Neither disagree nor agree
4. Somewhat agree
5. Strongly agree

How would you rate _____?

1. Lower than low
2. Low
3. Medium
4. High
5. Perfection

Circle the number that best represents your feeling about _____?

Well organized	6	5	4	3	2	1	Disorganized
Interesting	6	5	4	3	2	1	Boring
Valuable	6	5	4	3	2	1	Worthless
Excellent	6	5	4	3	2	1	Poor

Please rate how useful this program was for you.

Not at all useful
Somewhat useful
Very useful

How important is it to you to _____?

Very important
Somewhat important
Little importance
Not needed

Sometimes participants choose the neutral value more often. If this is a concern, the scale can be designed to run from one to four, so there is no middle choice. It is also useful to include a "no answer" (NA) option for participants who may not be informed enough to voice an opinion or an "other" option for participants who might want to present alternative answers. For questionnaires that consist almost entirely of close-ended responses, it can be effective to collect data using a tablet computer using software like FileMaker Pro, Qualtrics, or Google Forms. This will save you the work of copying pencil and paper responses into a computer and will ideally reduce transcription errors.

The largest difference between qualitative and quantitative approaches to questionnaires is how the results are presented. For qualitative questions, the researcher either summarizes general trends in narrative form, giving verbatim examples of different responses to show the range of responses or categorizes the responses given to identify patterns and trends across all participants. In quantitative questions, the results are categorized, described, and often analyzed using statistical tests. For examples, see Figures 7.2 and 7.3. Combining qualitative and quantitative approaches in the same questionnaire can also be used to uncover general trends while gaining insight into individual differences.

WEB QUESTIONNAIRES

Perhaps the biggest development in survey methodologies during the last decade is the collection of data through self-administered online

World of Viruses Survey

1. Where can viruses be found? (check all that apply)
   ___ in animals   ___ in plants   ___ in the soil
   ___ in the air   ___ in the ocean   ___ other (please describe):_____

2. Describe a virus (what is it and what does it do?).

3. How, if at all, can viruses be helpful?

4. Of the images below, circle the one(s) that you think are viruses.

5. Please explain why you chose the image(s) you circled.

6. How do viruses make you sick? Please explain your answer.

7. Describe, as best you can, how modern-day vaccinations help prevent disease.

8. What question(s) would you ask a virus expert to learn more about viruses?

9. What is your age? _____ years	10. What is your sex? Female Male	
11. Select the ethnic category with which you most closely identify:	12. Select one or more racial category with which you most closely identify:	
Hispanic or Latino	Not Hispanic or Latino	White		Asian
		American Indian or Alaska Native	Native Hawaiian or Other Pacific Islander	Black or African American

Thank you for your responses!

Figure 7.2   Front-end survey about viruses for high school-aged youth in libraries developed by Amy Spiegel, evaluator for the NIH-funded World of Viruses project.

Visitor Survey on Global Warming

The Koshland needs your help! We're updating our global warming exhibition and we want to hear your thoughts. Please fill out this survey, which will take 5-10 minutes to complete. Your comments are anonymous.

Your Visit to the Koshland Museum

1. On average, how often do you visit museums with science-related exhibits each year?

☐ Rarely
☐ 1-2 times a year
☐ 3-5 times a year
☐ 6 or more times a year

2. Select the statement that best describes your main reason for visiting the Museum today? (Select one.)

☐ I like the type of things I can learn here.
☐ I wanted to bring a friend or family member here.
☐ I discover things about myself when I am here.
☐ It was on my list of places to visit in DC.
☐ It relates to my professional interests and/or hobbies.
☐ Someone else suggested I come here.
☐ Another reason:
   Please describe _____

3. Before visiting today, did you know that an exhibit related to global warming would be here?

☐ No
☐ Yes
☐ Unsure

4. Before visiting today, did you go to *Global Warming Facts and Our Future* on the Koshland website?

☐ No
☐ Yes
☐ Unsure

Learning about Global Warming

5. Whose actions do you think are the most important for stopping global warming? (Select only one.)

☐ Individuals
☐ Government
☐ Industry leaders

6. From the list below, select 3 (or fewer) sources you most trust for information **about global warming**:

☐ Local political figures (mayors, governors)
☐ Major newspapers (Washington Post, New York Times)
☐ Private sector research scientists (energy companies)
☐ Museums and science centers
☐ Environmental activist organizations (Greenpeace, Sierra Club)
☐ Internet sources
☐ National political figures (president, congress)
☐ Public radio (NPR)
☐ Non-governmental organizations (World Wildlife Federation, National Academy of Sciences)
☐ Television sources
☐ Government scientists & researchers (NASA, EPA)

☐ I do not trust information from these sources.

7. From the list below, select 3 (or fewer) sources that you access most often for information **about global warming**:

☐ Local political figures (mayors, governors)
☐ Major newspapers (Washington Post, New York Times)
☐ Private sector research scientists (energy companies)
☐ Museums and science centers
☐ Environmental activist organizations (Greenpeace, Sierra Club)
☐ Internet sources
☐ National political figures (president, congress)
☐ Public radio (NPR)
☐ Non-governmental organizations (World Wildlife Federation, National Academy of Sciences)
☐ Television sources
☐ Government scientists & researchers (NASA, EPA)

☐ I do not access information from these sources.

Figure 7.3   Front-end survey on global warming developed by Heimlich, Koepfler, & Yocco (2010) for the Marian Koshland Science Museum of the National Academy of Sciences.

(Learning about Global Warming, cont'd)

Please indicate to what extent you agree with the following statements:

	Strongly DISAGREE						Strongly AGREE
I am very interested in learning about topics and issues related to global warming.	1	2	3	4	5	6	7
I am very knowledgeable about topics and issues related to global warming.	1	2	3	4	5	6	7
I believe global warming is a very serious problem.	1	2	3	4	5	6	7
I believe global warming requires immediate action.	1	2	3	4	5	6	7

Your Thoughts about Global Warming

Please indicate to what extent you agree with the following statements that relate to global warming:

	Strongly DISAGREE						Strongly AGREE
I think global warming is too big an issue for my actions to impact it.	1	2	3	4	5	6	7
I am willing to help stop global warming by supporting relevant organizations financially.	1	2	3	4	5	6	7
I can do little to reduce or stop global warming.	1	2	3	4	5	6	7
I can influence local officials to do something about global warming by sending letters, e-mails, or calling.	1	2	3	4	5	6	7
I am willing to help stop global warming by volunteering my time to relevant organizations.	1	2	3	4	5	6	7
I am willing to make personal changes to help stop global warming.	1	2	3	4	5	6	7
My local government has no role in resolving the issue of global warming.	1	2	3	4	5	6	7
Who I vote for in government impacts how global warming can be resolved.	1	2	3	4	5	6	7
I cannot affect the government's actions related to global warming.	1	2	3	4	5	6	7
I don't worry about global warming because we will develop new technologies to deal with it.	1	2	3	4	5	6	7

Figure 7.3   (Continued)

Global Warming and You

For each statement, place an "X" in the box that BEST FITS your answer. (Select only one response per statement.) For example, if you are aware of something, but don't do it, you would place an X under "I am aware of it". If you've been thinking about doing it, but haven't started yet, you would place an X under "I've been thinking about doing this."

	I would never do this	I am aware of this	I think this is a good idea	I used to do this	I am not able to do this	I've been thinking about doing this	I plan to do this soon	I do this: occasionally	I do this: frequently
I recycle things, such as bottles, cans, and newspapers.	☐	☐	☐	☐	☐	☐	☐	☐	☐
I look for information about global warming on TV, in print, or on the Internet.	☐	☐	☐	☐	☐	☐	☐	☐	☐
I talk to others about the importance of the issue of global warming.	☐	☐	☐	☐	☐	☐	☐	☐	☐
I use other means of transportation besides a car to reduce carbon emissions.	☐	☐	☐	☐	☐	☐	☐	☐	☐
I purchase foods produced locally, within a 100 mile radius of my house.	☐	☐	☐	☐	☐	☐	☐	☐	☐
I reduce my meat intake to two times a week to help reduce global warming.	☐	☐	☐	☐	☐	☐	☐	☐	☐
I purchase appliances that are friendly to the environment, such as EnergyStar.	☐	☐	☐	☐	☐	☐	☐	☐	☐
I buy fewer consumer goods to reduce waste.	☐	☐	☐	☐	☐	☐	☐	☐	☐
I turn the thermostat down by at least 2 degrees in the winter to conserve energy.	☐	☐	☐	☐	☐	☐	☐	☐	☐

Tell Us More about Yourself

This information helps the Museum know if it is serving diverse communities.

11. Are you:

☐ Female   ☐ Prefer not to answer
☐ Male

12. What year were you born? (ex. 1982)

____ ____ ____ ____ year

13. What is the highest level of education you have completed?

☐ High School   ☐ Prefer not to answer
☐ College
☐ Graduate degree or higher
☐ Other: _____

14. Where do you currently live?

☐ Local (inside the beltway)
☐ Neighboring state to DC (includes MD, VA)
☐ Other State (not neighboring to DC)
☐ Another country, please describe:
_____

Thank you so much for taking the time to complete this survey.
Enjoy your visit!

Figure 7.3   (Continued)

questionnaires. By using software such as Survey Monkey, Qualtrics, Google Forms, or Vovici, it is possible to design web-based questionnaires that eliminate the need for pencil-and-paper administration. According to Dillman, Smyth & Christian (2014), web-based questionnaires provide capabilities beyond those available for any other type of self-administered questionnaire.

As with paper-and-pencil questionnaires, however, web-based questionnaires require several important design considerations (Dillman, Smyth & Christian 2014):

- The welcome screen should be motivational, emphasize the ease of responding, and instruct participants about how to move to the next page. Keep in mind that some participants may have limited experience with how to answer a web-based questionnaire and perhaps even how to operate a computer or tablet for this express purpose. It is important that participants be informed of what action(s) will allow them to go to the first set of questions.
- Should written informed consent be required, there should be a page that clearly explains the full procedures for this process and actively forces participants to demonstrate consent before proceeding.
- Keep graphics and design simple. Depending on the operating system that participants are using, it is possible that questions may appear differently for them. The more complex the design, the greater the likelihood that variations may exist for participants.
- Provide specific instructions on how to take each necessary computer action to respond to a question. For instance, how do participants access the drop-down menu of answer choices? Do they use the mouse, keyboard stroke, or touchscreen to check a box? Although seemingly simple for experienced computer users, these actions are not necessarily universally understood and may result in participants abandoning the questionnaire.
- Consider using graphical indications of where the participant is in the completion process (i.e., Question 4 of 30), so that they can estimate how far they are from the end.
- All questionnaires, including those administered through the web, require trial testing with test participants to make sure that the instructions and questions are clearly understood.

Chapter 8

Presenting and Analyzing Data

We have discussed designing an evaluation study, measuring learning, and choosing methods for data collection. In this chapter, we turn to the process of presenting and analyzing data. Thinking through what you want to do with your data from the outset will ensure that decisions made along the way are consistent with your goals and allow you to represent data in the clearest and most useful manner.

If you have collected quantitative data, the analysis most often will involve the use of graphs, tables, and statistical techniques to summarize and describe your findings. If you collected qualitative data, then the analysis of your findings will most likely involve descriptive text, direct quotes, verbatim descriptions, drawings, photographs, and other materials to represent and reinforce major themes. Frequently, evaluation studies use both quantitative and qualitative methods, and the presentation and analysis of the data may include both descriptive text and statistical treatments.

EXPLORING AND GRAPHING DATA

Data analysis should begin with what Tukey (1977) termed *exploratory data analysis* (EDA). The goal of EDA is to learn about the data through the construction of charts, tables, figures, or lists. EDA can give you a sense of what the data show before conducting confirmatory statistical tests. For example, if you want to understand the amount of time visitors spend at an exhibit, then graphing the data points can reveal patterns that a simple average of the number of minutes spent at the exhibit could not express. For example, a graph might show that most visitors spend only a few minutes, but that some spend over an hour.

Graphing Data

The most common way of presenting quantitative data for EDA is to plot them on a graph so the patterns in the data can be made visually apparent. The choice of graph depends on the nature of the underlying data. Bar graphs are the simplest approach. The vertical axis shows the magnitude of the dependent variable, whereas the horizontal axis represents the categories of the independent variable.

A bar graph is called a *histogram* when the categories form a continuous series along a single dimension and the bar heights represent the number or proportion of observations in each category. Histograms are useful because they display details of the distribution of a variable (Figure 8.1). Line graphs place single data points to show trends in continuous data. In Figure 8.2, the occurrence of behaviors at exhibits is plotted over the course of an entire museum visit. A scatter plot, shown in Figure 8.3, illustrates the relationships between two continuously distributed variables.

Another kind of graph is called a *pie chart*. This type should be used only when the data represents parts of a whole, as in the case of percentages. Tufte (1983) and others generally do not recommend that pie charts be used because they contain relatively small amounts of data compared to other kinds of graphs and tables, and they can be perceptually deceptive because they fail to order numbers along a single visual dimension. The data that pie charts communicate can usually be shared more effectively in a table or simply in the text.

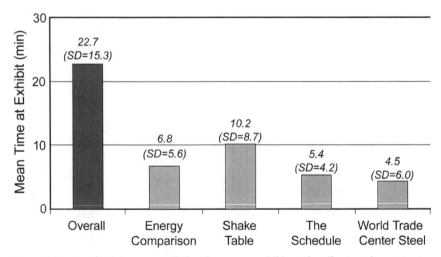

Figure 8.1   Graph of time spent in the Skyscraper exhibit at the Liberty Science Center designed by the Institute for Learning Innovation. *Source*: Liberty Science Center, Division of Exhibitions & Featured Experiences, Jersey City, NJ.

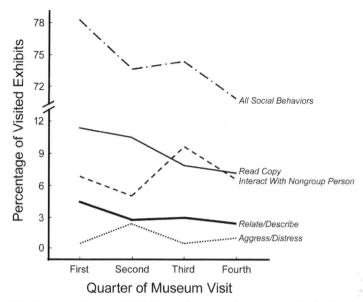

Figure 8.2 Graph by Diamond (1986) showing mean frequencies of behaviors over the course of visits of 81 people in 28 family groups to the Exploratorium and the Lawrence Hall of Science.

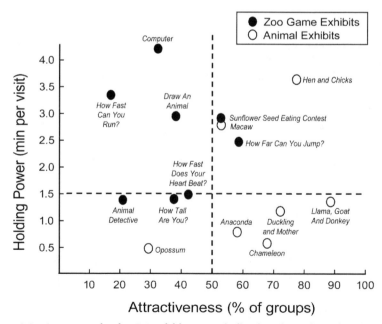

Figure 8.3 A scatter plot by Rosenfeld (1982) indicating the rating of various zoo exhibits by "holding power" and "attractiveness."

Graphs that communicate well take planning and organization. The legend, if used, should be clear and concise, including a title, a brief description of the data, and the number of participants, if applicable. In reports, graphs should be identified by figure number, with the number and legend always placed *beneath* the graph (note that the number and legend always go *above* a table).

Graphs should be understandable without additional information from the text. When you complete a graph, show it to someone who is not familiar with the subject matter. That person should be able to interpret it just on the basis of what is presented in the graph and the legend. Kosslyn (2006) presents a thorough review of how to create well-designed data graphs. According to Cleveland (1985), graphing data should be an iterative, experimental process. He suggests some guiding principles:

- Make the data stand out. Use visually prominent graphical statements to show the data, so that interesting features of the graph are obvious. Do not clutter the data region by overdoing the number of data labels, notes, keys, or marks.
- Put keys and markers just outside the data region and put notes in the legend or in the text. Keep the graph clear enough so that the information is preserved when the size is reduced or it is reproduced.
- The scale of a graph is the ruler along which we graph the data. Choose the scales so that the data fill up as much of the data region as possible. Tick marks indicate the scale like the inch marks on a ruler. Choose the range of tick marks to include or nearly include the range of data, but do not overdo the number of tick marks. Put tick marks outside of the data region. Choose comparable scales when two graphs are to be compared.
- It is not necessary for zero to always be included on a scale showing magnitude. If you do use zero, make sure the axis line will not obscure the data points. If this appears to be an issue, then move the zero slightly along the axis so the data points will be easy to see.
- Use a scale break only when necessary. If a break cannot be avoided, do not connect numerical values on two sides of a break.

SUMMARIZING DATA IN TABLES

Tables can be a useful way to summarize data for a report. Tables do not replace graphs because they rarely can communicate complex patterns and trends in data. Tables have the advantage, however, that they can include all the data on a particular topic. Tables are also the best way to show exact numerical values, so they work well when the data presentation requires many localized comparisons, and they are preferable to graphs for many small data sets (Tufte 1997). Large tables are generally relegated to appendices or supplementary material and are usually not included in shorter, summary reports.

There are instances, however, when tables are useful, even essential. When statistical tests have been performed on the data, a table can provide a condensed summary of the findings or can summarize general themes. Tables can also make comparisons, summarize the results of a questionnaire or an interview item, or summarize a single feature from an observational study (see examples in Tables 8.1, 8.2, and 8.3).

Tables require just as careful thought and organization as do graphs. For example, tables should be listed as "Table (number)" and should include a title. The legend, if used, should provide a brief description of the data. Statistical tests performed on the data may or may not be included in the table legend. The table number and the legend should be placed at the top of the

Table 8.1   The responses of former Exploratorium Explainers to the following: *After you stopped working in the Exploratorium, we'd like to know in what ways being an explainer affected your life. To what extent did the Explainer program have impact on you?* **Comparisons among groups were made using analysis of variance. Significant differences among groups are indicated below (Diamond et al. 1987: 649).**

	Percent (High Impact) (N = 116)	Rated Impact (Mean and SD)
Measures of Program Impact on Science and Learning		
Your curiosity about how things work	80	4.2 (0.9)
Your interest in science	67	3.8 (1.2)
Your confidence that you could understand science	66	3.8 (1.2)
The amount you watch science programs on TV or listen to them on the radio	35	2.8 (1.4)
The amount you read about science or scientists	32	3.0 (1.2)
The number of science courses you took or plan to take in school or college	32	2.9 (1.4)*
*Measures of Program Impact on Communication and Self-Esteem**		
Your ability to teach people	80	4.2 (0.9)
Your desire to work with people	73	4.0 (1.0)
Your desire to learn on your own	63	3.7 (1.1)
Your understanding of your capabilities	62	3.7 (0.9)
Your self-confidence	60	3.9 (0.9)
Your effectiveness in other jobs	50	3.7 (1.1)

Reprinted with permission of John Wiley & Sons, Inc.
* Ratings of students indicating a high interest in science in high school were significantly higher ($p < .001$) than other students.
** Ratings of female Explainers on factor 2 were significantly higher ($p < 0.03$) than the rating of male explainers on this factor.

Table 8.2   Categories of adjectives used by visitors in conversations while at the Shedd Aquarium (Serrell 1977, p. 51).

	Adjectives Selected by Visitors to Describe Aquarium Visit*	
	Visit was (%)	*Visit Should be (%)*
Informative	49	58
Entertainment	47	45
Educational	47	60
Recreation	34	25
Looking at an exhibit	16	7
Disappointing	1	–

*Totals exceed 100% because of multiple choices.

Table 8.3   Length of stops by visitors to the Mankind Discovering Gallery at the Royal Ontario Museum (Alt & Griggs 1989, p. 20).

Length of Stop	*Percentage of Total Stops*
Up to 5 seconds	18
6–10 seconds	28
11–30 seconds	31
Over 30 seconds	23

Note: Table based on a sample of 100 respondents. Reprinted Courtesy Royal Ontario Museum.

table. Always refer to the table in the text, so the reader's attention is directed to the table at the appropriate time.

Do not try to put so much information in a table that it becomes difficult to read. Several shorter, simpler tables are often more desirable than one complex one. Tables should not require more than a few minutes to read and comprehend. The text should be large enough so a magnifying glass will not be required for average readers. Remember that the report may be copied or printed. Do not use colors or close shades that could be confused on a black-and-white copy.

There are general principles that apply to any kind of data display. Tufte (1983, p. 183) summarizes the elements that make up "friendly" or easy-to-use data graphics from those that are difficult to use. Friendly tables and graphs have the following characteristics:

- Words are spelled out; mysterious and elaborate encoding is avoided.
- Words run from left to right (not up and down), the usual directions for reading occidental languages.
- Little messages help to explain the data.

- Elaborately encoded shadings, cross-hatching, and colors are avoided; instead, labels are placed on the graphic itself. No legend is required.
- Graphic attracts viewers, provokes curiosity.
- Colors, if used, are chosen so the color-deficient and color-blind (5 to 10 percent of viewers) can make sense of the graphic. Most color-deficient people can distinguish blue from other colors.
- Type is clear, precise, and modest.
- Type is uppercase and lowercase, with serifs.

Unfriendly graphics have the following features:

- Abbreviations abound, requiring the viewer to sort through text to decode.
- Words run vertically, particularly along the Y-axis; words run in several different directions.
- Graphic is cryptic, requires repeated references to scattered text.
- Obscure coding requires going back and forth between legend and graphic.
- Graphic is filled with unnecessary and distracting decorations (chart junk).
- Design is insensitive to color-deficient viewers; red and green are used for essential contrasts.
- Type is too closely spaced (clotted) or too large, elaborate, and distracting.
- Type is all capitals, sans serif.

COMPARING DATA SETS

To learn more about the details of data analysis, including the nuts and bolts of statistical computation, you should refer to an introductory statistics text. In this section, we provide a brief overview of the considerations involved in selecting a method of analysis.

The first steps are to decide what kinds of data you have and what kinds of questions you want to ask of it. There are three types of quantitative data that are collected in informal educational studies: counts, measures, and ratios. A count is simply the number of times that something occurred or the number of subjects in a particular category. Examples might be the number of females aged between 20 and 30 that visited a museum during a particular period or the number of questions asked of a volunteer. Counts are always integers, meaning they are whole numbers greater than or equal to zero.

Measures are variables that result from using a measuring device, such as a yardstick or stopwatch. Distance and time are the most common measures:

How far away do visitors stand from an exhibit or from each other? How long do they spend at each exhibit?

The third type of data is a ratio. A ratio can be the number of times a visitor looked at the graphics throughout the course of their visit, divided by the total number of exhibits visited. When the ratio is between two counts or two measures of the same type, it is called a *proportion* or *percentage*. An example is the percentage of people that answered "yes" to an interview question. Whether your data is a count, measure, or percentage will influence the type of statistical tests that you can use.

Descriptive Statistics

Once you have determined the type of data you will be collecting, the next step in planning the analysis is to decide how to use descriptive statistics. *Descriptive statistics* are empirical summaries of the data; they are single values or small sets of values that provide summary information about the entire data set. There are two kinds of descriptive statistics: measures of *central tendency* and measures of *variability*.

Central tendency refers to the average value. There are three commonly used measures of central tendency:

- *Mean*: The most common estimate of the center of a distribution is the mean, or arithmetic average, of the distribution. The values of the variable are added across all observations, and the sum is divided by the number of observations.
- *Median*: The median is the value of the observation that forms the midpoint of a distribution: Half of the data fall below the median, and the other half fall above it. Medians are preferable to means as descriptors when the data are not normally distributed.
- *Mode*: The mode is the most common number in the data set. The mode is often used when dividing numbers to obtain a mean would not make sense, because the value needs to be an integer. Modes are only informative when there is no obvious central tendency in the distribution and when one value (the mode) is far more abundant than the others.

Variability

The central tendency is an important characteristic of a data set, but it is not sufficient to fully describe the data. Consider two simple data sets (a) 10, 20, 30, 40, 50 and (b) 28, 29, 30, 31, 32. Both data sets have the same mean: 30. But the mean does not adequately describe the two data sets; they differ substantially in terms of *variability*. In data set (a), each of the values is much farther from the mean of 30 than in data set (b). Knowing how variable a data set is important because it can tell us how much each value is like (or unlike) the mean.

A primary measure of variability is the *standard deviation*. The *standard deviation* is a measure of how a set of measurements varies from the mean. It is the average deviation of each observation in the distribution from the mean.

Representing Central Tendency and Variability: Normal Distribution or Bell Curve

When the same measurement is taken repeatedly, the values obtained will not all be identical. Because of random factors, successive measurements will usually differ from each other. If the measurements are taken of different subjects or of the same subject at different times, the variability will be even larger. But with enough repetitions, the random factors will average out, producing a distribution that is shaped rather like a bell, in that values close to the middle are more common than values that are much higher or lower. If the data are normally distributed, the peak of the bell will be close to the mean, and the standard deviation will be the average of the distances from the mean.

Inferential Statistics

After exploring and describing the data that have been collected, the next step is to determine whether the results we have observed are *statistically significant*. This determines whether the differences between groups are larger than might be expected by chance alone. It can be surprising how many differences can be the result of sheer chance when, for example, more return museum visitors end up in an experimental group than in the control group. In this case, differences between the experimental group and the control group could be due to error in sampling, rather than a real or meaningful difference in behavior. To determine whether the results exceed what would be expected by chance alone, researchers often conduct what is called *inferential statistical tests*. The inference is based on whether the result exceeds what would be expected by chance alone, and whether the result is likely to replicate if the same experiment were conducted with a different sample.

Several factors influence whether the observed differences will be statistically significant. One obvious factor is the magnitude of the difference in central tendency between the two groups; the larger the difference, the more likely the difference is to be statistically significant. In addition, the size of the sample also affects statistical significance; a larger sample is more likely to yield a reliable result and a statistically significant difference. Finally, the variability in the two groups will also affect statistical significance. If the standard deviations are high, it will be harder to show that the difference is statistically significant.

Statistical analysis is mainly designed to address three types of questions: questions about distributions, questions about magnitudes, and questions about association. There are many kinds of statistical tests, and their use depends on the type of data and what questions you plan to ask about the data. A few commonly used statistical tests are as follows:

- *Chi-squared test*: This is a common technique for comparing two or more distributions of counts. It relies on taking a sum of differences between levels of a variable of interest across categories. It is particularly valuable for analyzing responses to questionnaires or multiple-choice tests.
- *Analysis of variance* or *Student's t-test*: These tests compare distributions of counts or measures by using the means and standard deviations of each distribution. If there are only two categories being contrasted, compare them using the Student's t-test; if there are more than two contrasting groups, then use analysis of variance.
- *Correlation*: This technique compares associations between measures or ratios. The straight line that best describes the relationship between the two variables is computed, yielding an estimate of the degree of influence of one variable on the other. This measure, the correlation coefficient, is equal to one when the two variables rise and fall simultaneously. It is equal to negative one when high levels of one variable are associated with low levels of the other. When there is no meaningful association between variables, the correlation coefficient is zero. From knowledge of the correlation coefficient and the sample size, you can make statements of a varying degree of confidence about the relationship between the variables.

QUALITATIVE DATA

The methods of dealing with qualitative data are more diverse than quantitative methods. This section highlights some of the important issues and processes relating to qualitative data analysis. For a detailed discussion of the various steps involved, we recommend Miles, Huberman, & Saldaña (2013). As these authors point out, qualitative data analysis involves three iterative and concurrent phases: (1) data reduction, (2) data displays, and (3) conclusion drawing and verification. Across all three phases, the analysis process needs to be well documented because, unlike its quantitative counterpart, qualitative analysis has no formula or fixed rules.

Data Reduction

Data reduction is the process of selecting, focusing, simplifying, abstracting, and transforming the data that appear in written-up field notes or transcriptions. During this process, the evaluator makes decisions about what in the data set is important, which patterns are most relevant to the questions and issues at hand, and what story the data tell. Data reduction does not necessarily mean quantifying or counting patterns or trends within the data. Although this can sometimes be useful, it is important in qualitative analysis to keep in mind the larger context in which the data collection occurred.

Data reduction often takes the form of coding. *Codes* are tags or labels for assigning meaning to the information compiled during a study. Codes are usually attached to "chunks" of varying size—words, phrases, sentences, or whole paragraphs—connected or unconnected to a specific setting. By assigning codes to the data, the evaluator organizes it and begins to make meaning from it. The creation of codes can be either deductive or inductive. Using a *deductive* approach, the evaluator generates a list of possible codes from the outset of the study, using the conceptual framework or research questions to guide the process. An *inductive* approach is more open ended, allowing codes to emerge from the data at hand, and assuming a more context-sensitive process.

Coding is the process of classifying respondents' answers or comments. People may say similar things in different ways. For example, one respondent might say, "I really liked the dinosaur exhibit," and another might say, "The dinosaur exhibit was one of my favorites." These two quotes are not identical, but there is a core similarity: Both indicate that the visitors liked the dinosaur visit. The goal of the coding process would be to identify these sorts of similarities and to treat them as similar in the data analysis. In this example, both cases would be assigned the same code, perhaps "liked exhibit." Coding provides a way for researchers to make sense of the complex and different ways in which people express their attitudes, beliefs, or goals.

As mentioned previously, behaviors can also be coded. For example, if we observe visitors' behaviors in an exhibit, we might code whether they talked with their children, talked with an adult, or remained silent. The codes would give the evaluator a way to concisely summarize what might otherwise be an intractably large amount of data.

Coding always involves judgments about what behaviors or responses should be treated as similar. It is important that the coding system be *reliable*, meaning that two people, coding independently, should come to similar conclusions about the codes for any given behavior or response. Developing reliable codes is often challenging, but it is important that all coders agree as closely as possible. The evaluator should develop clear definitions of each code and provide clear examples, including video examples where possible. It is also important that coders work independently and keep notes of decisions that they found difficult. These difficult decisions should then be discussed among the group.

Several software programs exist that are useful for coding and organizing large amounts of qualitative data. Most programs permit the evaluator to work from existing transcripts or field notes to assign codes to selective chunks of the data and then sort the data in varying ways according to those codes. The software can assist the researcher in drawing links between themes in transcripts that might otherwise be difficult to find. Moreover, some software can even process text automatically on the basis of key words or patterns of use, although this kind of software is rarely a substitute for a careful reading or viewing of the data. Video coding software allows the researcher to define codes, implement them as pull-down menus, and then assign codes to particular segments of the video. Coding video without this kind of software can be a cumbersome and slow process.

Data Displays

Typically, qualitative data is presented in the form of extended text, using narrative description of key phenomenon and relying heavily on participant quotations where possible. Quotations are used to provide examples or illustrations of more general principles. They can show common patterns in how visitors feel about and interpret their environment. Quotations can also be a powerful tool in demonstrating individual differences, emphasizing and appreciating the variability among visitors in informal educational settings.

Quotations can be used in a variety of different ways. The question-and-answer form is useful when the interviewer's presence sets a needed context. According to Brady (1977), the question-and-answer form gives readers precise answers to basic questions about complex issues, and it provides a clear window, allowing the subject to speak directly to the reader. However, even question-and-answer formats can sometimes be ambiguous. The following includes an excerpt from an interview with a famous prizefighter immediately after a fight (Brady 1977, p. 208):

> *"Did he hit you hard?"*

> *"Holy Jesus!"*

> *"Do you want to fight him again?"*

> *"Holy Jesus!"*

> *"Do you think you could lick him if you fought him again?"*

"Holy Jesus!"

"Does your head hurt?"

"Holy Jesus!"

When quotations are paraphrased, it is often difficult to keep the original feeling. Paraphrased quotations are also sometimes deliberately misrepresented. Brady describes the interviewer's astonishment when he read how a reporter had paraphrased the preceding conversation: "Max's blows were very hard. He hurt me several times—I'll have to admit that. But I sincerely believe I could defeat him and I would like to have another chance . . ."

On the other hand, Spock uses indirect quotations very effectively in the following example:

> The anecdote that I think is perhaps most exciting is the one in which Steven Jay Gould talks about his first visit to the American Museum in New York. It wasn't just the Yankees that imprinted him, but it was the Tyrannosaurus that he saw on his first visit. He talks about that as a pivotal point in his life. He says that at age five or six, when he first saw the Tyrannosaurus, he knew that he was going to do something for the rest of his life related to that experience. It made a difference to Gould; it got him going and thinking about dinosaurs and then paleontology and then evolution; and evolution was the thing he ended up studying. I also think that the drama of this event has something to do with the fact that Gould has a deep commitment to popularization, for which he gets a lot of criticism from his colleagues. (Spock 1988, p. 257)

Direct quotations are often the most effective way of conveying a visitor's experience. Diamond and her colleagues obtained the following quotations from a series of in-depth interviews of high school-aged Explainers working at the Exploratorium in San Francisco, California. They asked the Explainers to talk about how the museum program influenced them:

> I grew. I grew up here. I had a lot of prejudiced views. I was raised in a traditional Chinese family that has a prejudice against blacks. There was one person here I was particularly attached to. She broke down a lot of deep barriers. She taught me everyone has a veneer, and to break through that veneer is to take each person as a soul. Wilson, Explainer in 1979. (Diamond et al. 1987, p. 647)
>
> I used to tolerate a lot of my own mistakes. On the floor you fall on your face a lot in front of those that know better. Once at an eye dissection, I got into a conversation with an ophthalmology student. I'd be explaining things but all of a sudden I was learning new stuff by talking to this guy. Gabe, Explainer in 1981. (Diamond et al. 1987, p. 647)

McManus often uses direct quotations from her recording of visitor conversations in museums:

> visitors sometimes talked back to the "museum someone" who was communicating with them . . . In one transcript, the visitor reads aloud: "Are you a primate? Yes, you are a primate," Then he answers out loud, "NO I'M NOT." (McManus 1989b, p. 5)

Verification in qualitative evaluation can take many forms. It may involve the evaluator remaining open to alternate interpretations and returning to the data multiple times to check the underlying assumptions. In this case, the evaluator might revisit the analysis process and map out the links between the data, coding, and interpretation, noting where different interpretations might be made or where there are gaps in the interpretation—such as when some data have not been taken into account.

Alternately, verification may be more elaborate, involving colleagues who are asked to review coding processes and examine resulting interpretations. This process minimizes researcher bias, in which one evaluator may look at data through a particular lens, while missing other possible interpretations. For example, two evaluators may first independently draft an initial analysis of qualitative data and then come together to verify their interpretations and develop conclusions collaboratively. Member checks can also be useful ways of verifying qualitative data and involve asking participants themselves to review and comment on your interpretations of the data. For example, in an evaluation focused on a community's attitudes and perceptions of a topic, the evaluator would share their initial interpretations and gather feedback from participants before making final conclusions. When using member checks, it is extremely important to share the interpretation at a stage when the evaluator is still fully open to making changes.

Part III

EVALUATING DIGITAL MEDIA: OPPORTUNITIES AND PITFALLS

Digital technology has come to play a larger role in informal learning institutions of all kinds. Not only do visitors bring smartphones, tablets, and even smartwatches with them on visits, but exhibit designers are also exploring a proliferation of technology to create new interactive exhibit elements. For people who care deeply about informal learning experiences, these changes are exhilarating and unnerving at the same time. Even the placement of a simple QR code next to a diorama in a natural history museum creates a rudimentary link between physical reality of the museum gallery and a vast digital world of the web and social media. This kind of link also leaves a digital trace of the visitor experience. Computer log data might tell us how many people scanned the QR code, what they looked at on a corresponding web page, and possibly even *who* they were. All of this opens new possibility for evaluating learning while raising important questions about the role of traditional static exhibits in a digital era. What does this mean for informal learning experiences and the ways in which we evaluate their effectiveness? What ethical issues should we be concerned about? And how can digital technology best be used to enhance rather than to detract from visitor learning?

The good news is that evaluating digital interactive exhibits is more or less the same as evaluating any other type of exhibit. All the same principles apply, and you do not need a technical background to use the tools and methods described in other parts of this book to understand how well a digital experience is working. In fact, being an effective evaluator means that we must look beyond the superficial shine of new technology to see the underlying visitor experience for what it really is. But, there are some special considerations and valuable tools that can augment other standard evaluation approaches. In particular, digital interactive exhibits can be used to automate many aspects of the data collection process, providing new tools to answer fundamental evaluation questions in new ways.

Chapter 9

The Shifting Landscape of Digital Interactive Exhibits

This chapter will focus on evaluating digital interactive exhibits that are meant to be experienced, at least in part, at a museum or other informal learning institutions. There are, of course, many mobile technologies that are blurring the line between museums and other learning settings such as homes, schools, and out-of-school programs, but these are beyond the scope of this chapter. We will start by looking at a variety of different digital interactive exhibits featuring technologies that are already in wide use, as well as those that are likely to play a role in the next five to ten years. Chapter 10 will then review popular methods and tools for evaluating digital interactive exhibits, with special considerations for working with audio, video, and screen capture recordings. This will include a discussion of tools for working with automated data collection, including computer logs, video capture, and embedded surveys and assessments.

WHAT WE MEAN BY "DIGITAL INTERACTIVES": A BROADENING OF SCOPE

Museums have indisputably entered an era of ubiquitous computing. The ways in which audiences engage with digital interactives have diversified wildly. This section gives examples of some of this diversity with the goal of providing some orienting ideas and vocabulary. A consistent theme with all of these developments is that the most compelling uses of digital technology all support learning by creating new ways for visitors to engage—with content and ideas, with other visitors, and with institutions as repositories of scientific and cultural knowledge.

Interactive Displays—Large and Small

In the last few years, touchscreen displays have become almost ubiquitous in informal environments, and they are used in many different ways. For example, smaller tablet displays have sometimes replaced static text labels as a way for visitors to learn more about exhibited objects or organisms. Chicago's Field Museum recently opened the Cyrus Tang Hall of China, a 7,500 square foot exhibit showcasing hundreds of artifacts accompanied by 45 interactive "digital reading rails." These rails are long, thin computer displays with information about artifacts on display. The designers worked hard to preserve the accessibility of traditional text labels while providing just the right amount of interactivity to open layers of additional information to interested visitors.

Museums also use much larger digital displays for a wide variety of interactive experiences, including learning games, exploration of multimedia content, and interaction with virtual 3D objects. Some of these displays are easily big enough for groups of several visitors to gather around and engage in shared activities. Larger displays can be mounted horizontally like a table, vertically like a whiteboard, or somewhere in between. An interesting use of large displays has been to give visitors the opportunities to explore abstract "information spaces" ranging from census data (Roberts et al. 2014) to large biological data sets. For example, the "Life on Earth" project has used biological databases with information on the relationships of hundreds of thousands of species to create an experience in which visitors can *fly* through hundreds of millions of years of evolutionary history (Figure 9.1; Block et al. 2012).

Similar efforts include the Living Liquid exhibit at the Exploratorium in the San Francisco Exploratorium (Ma, Liao, Ma, & Frazier 2012), in which

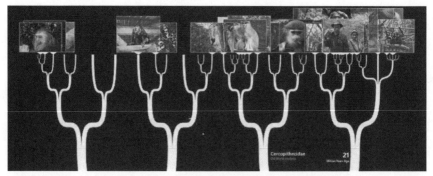

Figure 9.1 Screenshot from the NSF-funded DeepTree exhibit from the Life on Earth Project (Block et al. 2015; Davis et al. 2015; see https://lifeonearth.seas.harvard.edu).

visitors explore seasonal changes in plankton populations on a global scale, and the use of gigapixel deep zoom interfaces at the Carnegie Museum of Natural History (Louw & Crowley 2013).

Mixed Reality

Even though interactive displays seem to be growing in popularity, it is far from the consensus that informal learning environments should be over-run with computer screens. An alternative approach is to more seamlessly blend digital and physical worlds using *mixed reality* approaches. The term *mixed reality* is intended to capture a spectrum of visitor experiences. Virtual reality (VR) exhibits immerse visitors in 3D virtual worlds usually by using head-mounted displays. Here, the idea is to give visitors the experience of another world beyond what could be accessed easily or directly in real life. For example, visitors might take a walk on Mars or explore a remote archaeological site reconstructed to resemble its existence in the distant past. Rather than immersing visitors in a virtual world, augmented reality (AR) exhibits overlay digital information on top of the real world. This can be done with a secondary display, projectors, or even special glasses like Microsoft's HoloLens or Google Glass. In collaboration with the University of Pennsylvania, The Franklin Institute in Philadelphia, Pennsylvania, is exploring the use of AR to reveal the invisible phenomena behind several hands-on science learning experiences. In their Bernoulli Ball exhibit, for example, visitors can experience air pressure fluctuations around a levitated rubber ball while at the same time watching a real-time visual representation of the airflow around the ball on a computer screen (Yoon, Elinich, Wang, Steinmeier, & Tuckr 2012). One nice part about AR is that the computer interface is unobtrusive or completely absent—visitors manipulate physical exhibits, which are seamlessly augmented with digital effects.

Whole-Body Interaction

Somewhere between VR and AR are immersive, whole-body experiences, in which visitors use their hands, arms, or entire bodies to interact with digital simulations. A classic example is Snibbe's Boundary Functions exhibit, in which visitors use their bodies to interact with the mathematical construct of Voronoi diagrams (see Figure 9.2; Snibbe & Raffle 2009).

Another excellent example is the Fly Like a Pterosaur exhibit at the American Museum of Natural History, New York, in which visitors use their entire bodies to "pilot" two species of flying pterosaurs over prehistoric landscapes. Many learning researchers are now exploring the links between "embodied interaction" and the learning that these kinds of exhibits make possible.

Figure 9.2   Boundary Functions exhibit by Scott Snibbe (www.snibbe.com). *Source*: Photo courtesy of Scott Snibbe.

Tangible Interaction

"Tangible Interfaces" are another innovation that will become more common in museums. Similar to whole-body interaction, instead of using screen-based input devices (like mice, trackballs, or even touchscreens), visitors instead manipulate special-purpose physical objects that are tracked by a computer system. Tangibles help bring a hands-on feel to digital interactives that would otherwise be entirely screen based. They are increasingly popular as interactive tabletop displays have become more common; many of these displays can track a collection of physical objects along with visitor touch input. The Oztoc exhibit at the New York Hall of Science is an excellent example that combines screen-based effects with the manipulation of physical tiles representing components of electrical circuits (see Figure 9.3; Lyons et al. 2014).

Research has begun to show that tangibility of digital experiences can make a difference in terms of visitor experience. A study at the Museum of Science in Boston, Massachusetts, compared a computer programming and robotics exhibit that used a tangible interface to the same exhibit with a computer mouse. The researchers found that the tangible exhibit was more inviting to a broader range of visitors while simultaneously increasing the amount of collaborative interaction between participants (Horn et al. 2012). A more

Figure 9.3 Oztoc Exhibit at the New York Hall of Science. *Source*: Photo by Andrew Kelly/New York Hall of Science.

recent study at the Exploratorium in San Francisco came to similar conclusions in a comparison of tangible and multitouch interaction (Ma et al. 2015).

Proximity-Aware Systems

One technology that will undoubtedly transform evaluation in informal environments is proximity-aware tracking systems. Low-power wireless sensors can now be used to triangulate the position of visitors in a room with a fairly high degree of precision. As these and other technologies improve, it will be possible to collect a large amount of data about visitor movements through galleries, akin to the early work of Melton and Robinson (Melton 1933; Robinson 1931), but at a larger scale and at lower cost. It will also be possible to feed tracking information back into digital interactive exhibits to create personalized experiences in real time. Imagine an exhibit that was aware of what you had already seen on your visit and could respond accordingly. Of course, these tracking technologies raise ethical concerns related to privacy, and they also do not obviate the need for careful human observation of visitor activities in galleries.

Participatory Technologies

In an age of pervasive social media, researchers and practitioners are asking questions about the fundamental relationship between informal learning institutions and their visitors. One growing area of interest builds on the participatory nature of social media (Simon 2010). Social media services are thought of as *platforms* with the content created, in large part, by participants. Media is curated, critiqued, and repurposed by users as much as it is by any expert or "authority." From this perspective, visitors are seen as more than situated co-constructors of meaning; they are co-constructors with the institution, other visitors, and larger communities, of content and even of the museum itself. They are curators and commentators who help set the agenda of the institution.

These transformational ideas also raise important questions about how evaluation should be carried out, and even the nature of evaluation itself. Simon's (2010) book, *The Participatory Museum*, is an excellent reference for those interested in pursuing these questions further. He points out that exhibits can incorporate ideas or technologies directly from social media platforms as a way to engage visitors in more participatory experiences. One example is the Tangible Flags exhibit developed at the University of Maryland in collaboration with the National Park Service (Chipman, Drin, Beer, Fails, Guha, & Simms 2006). Children place colorful flags along the path of an outdoor nature walk to highlight things that they find interesting along the way. These flags contain wireless electronic tags that can be scanned by tablet computers that the kids carry with them on the walk. Kids use the tablet computers to draw pictures or ask questions about things that they are curious about. These digital annotations are tied physically to the flags' locations, and other visitors who come along later can scan the same flags and add their own thoughts and drawings to the original annotations.

What's Next?

All of these examples are really just scratching the surface. There are many other emerging subfields of computer science research that give us hints as to what is on the horizon for museums and other informal learning institutions. With that in mind, here are a few newer technologies to look for in the next five to ten years.

- *Brain-computer interfaces*: Researchers are developing low-cost, nonintrusive ways to monitor and respond to human brain activity. An excellent example of this is the Mindball exhibit at the Museum of Science and Industry in Chicago. Headbands monitor the brain activity of two visitors who compete to "out relax" their opponent.
- *Organic user interfaces* (OUI): OUI is a branch of human-computer interaction research concerned with advances in display technologies. We will soon see a variety of screens that are larger, lighter, and even flexible.

Imagine bending or folding a computer display as a means of interacting with an exhibit.

- *Human-biology interaction*: The Tech Museum of Innovation in San Jose, California, is collaborating with researchers at Stanford University to create experiences in which visitors interact with living microorganisms (Lee et al. 2015). Visitors use their hands to draw on a touchscreen displaying a microscope view of bacterial cells that react to specific colors of light. These drawings are projected directly into the petri dish, creating real-time interactions between visitors and bacteria.

SUMMARY

Technology will undoubtedly continue to evolve; what seems exotic today will seem commonplace tomorrow. As evaluators it is important to keep our attention focused on the experience of our audiences rather than the novelty of technology. If technology leads to enjoyable and engaging activities that help visitors understand the world in new ways, then it will stand the test of time. Many of the examples in this chapter are ten or more years old, but they are still compelling, because they create unique opportunities for visitors to engage together. The tools described in Part II are all well suited to the task of evaluating any of the experiences covered in this chapter. That said, because computers are involved in all of these experiences, there is the possibility of automating aspects of the data collection. Chapter 10 reviews tools and special considerations for working with digital interactive exhibits.

Chapter 10

Tools for Evaluating Digital Exhibits

The brief review of technology covered in Chapter 9 raises some important questions about the nature of evaluation in informal learning environments. With all of the possible changes brought about by new technology, are there also new tools and methods for assessing the quality of visitor experiences? And, are our essential guiding questions the same, or has the purpose of evaluation itself shifted with the technology? Despite the diversity of new technologies, the tools and methods for evaluating digital interactive exhibits remain largely the same as those covered in other chapters. Understanding the quality of visitor experiences is still fundamentally a human question. No amount of investment in technology on its own will guarantee that visitors had a good time, learned something new, or came away with a different perspective on an interesting topic. That said, there are some special considerations and new tools to keep in mind as you plan studies that involve digital exhibits. This chapter start by reviewing some common challenges and tips for working with audio and video data. We will then discuss starting points for working with computer-generated log data and other forms of automated data collection.

CHALLENGES AND TIPS FOR WORKING WITH AUDIO AND VIDEO

With many of the examples described in Chapter 9, the boundaries of digital interactive experiences have become blurry, broad, and distributed across time and space. Ubiquitous computing tends to emphasize more subtle forms of interaction that engage multiple visitors at the same time from different positions and perspectives. While this can help make exhibits more engaging, it can also make it more difficult to use audio and video recordings to capture and understand visitor experience.

An extreme example is the Connected Worlds exhibit at the New York Hall of Science. This is a room-sized exhibit with multiple large displays in which many visitors at a time use hand and arm gestures to interact with several virtual ecosystems that are connected by shared resources (such as a central supply of water). Capturing useful video and audio at such an exhibit is challenging to say the least. Visitors walk in and out of view while fluidly forming (and reforming) collaborative groups. Other visitors can interact with secondary displays showing a global view of the entire simulated ecosystem or simply watch from a distance. What are the boundaries of this experience? Who counts as a participant? And what are the effective ways to capture a diversity of visitor interaction? Just one video camera, whether mounted in a fixed location or held by a researcher or visitor, would be inadequate to capture many aspects of the larger collective experience. And, as if collecting video data were not problematic enough, the location of exhibits in a cavernous space with a great deal of ambient noise makes audio recording especially difficult.

Connected Worlds is an extreme example, but digital exhibits on a smaller scale pose similar challenges for audio and video recording. For example, one important decision is where to position video recording equipment relative to an exhibit. With large touchscreen displays, evaluators may want to capture both visitors' faces and the content of the screen that they are interacting with. Positioning the cameras behind visitors for an "over-the-shoulder" shot is good for viewing the exhibit display and visitors' hands and arms. But this angle misses out on faces, voices, and more subtle visitor-to-visitor interaction. Alternatively, positioning the camera on the other side of the display facing toward visitor solves some of these problems but misses out on the contents of the screen itself. Both these camera positions, over-the-shoulder and face-forward, also assume that visitors are interacting with content at a fixed orientation from one side of the display. But for many horizontal tabletops displays, visitors gather around all sides of the exhibit, making it impossible for any of the cameras to see everything in a single shot. Adding to these difficulties, limitations in dynamic range can make it difficult for a camera to simultaneously focus on bright computer displays and also on visitor faces and bodies in dimly lit galleries. The result is that the relative brightness of screens will often make visitors appear shadowlike in contrast (e.g., Figure 10.1).

One tempting alternative is to use several recording devices to capture multiple streams of video and audio simultaneously. For example, you might ask participants to wear a voice recorder on a lanyard and set up two

Figure 10.1   Connected Worlds at the New York Hall of Science created by Design I/O.
Source: Photo by David Handschuh/New York Hall of Science.

video cameras to capture different angles of the same exhibit. Wearable or handheld cameras are also increasingly reliable and inexpensive. These can be held or worn by visitors as a way to see the world from their perspective, which can be especially valuable when visitors are moving around a larger space.

While the use of multiple recording devices can be beneficial and often necessary, there are some important trade-offs to consider as you design your studies. Most importantly, multiple streams of video and audio on many different devices can be cumbersome to keep organized and tricky to synchronize for analysis purposes. A few tools such as ChronoVis from the University of California, San Diego, (http://chronoviz.com/) are specifically designed to work with multiple data sources including audio, video, and log data. But you will still have to organize all of the recording files, so it is worth thinking carefully about whether an extra camera or audio recorder will buy you a significant advantage for analysis. Also, keep in mind that giving visitors their own cameras will likely change their experience in substantial and unpredictable ways. For example, we have found that visitors will often adopt a documentary filmmaker persona when holding a camera, narrating their experience for an imagined audience. This might be appealing for analysis purposes (you get a running monologue of participant thinking), but it is unlikely to reflect the experience of most other visitors. There are, of course, also ethical considerations to keep in mind with visitor-held cameras, as you will have limited control over who and what visitors capture in their footage.

An alternative is to record directly from the computers that drive the interactive experience. Using software like Camtasia (available from TechSmith), you can merge live screen capture video with built-in front-facing cameras. This can be an excellent way to record visitor experiences from different perspectives while keeping media streams synchronized and bundled in a single file. It also solves some of the dynamic range issues mentioned above. Camtasia and similar screen capture software can be configured to record at low frame rates and low resolution, making it possible to run automated data capture for longer periods of time. Even if you cannot record directly from an interactive exhibit itself, you can achieve much the same result using a small laptop or tablet with a built-in web camera and external audio recording equipment.

NOTES ON AUDIO AND VIDEO EQUIPMENT

Although the quality of the video itself is an important factor, some of the most important issues relate to the size of captured video files and the means for storing and transferring them. Most modern cameras advertise that they can record in extremely high definition. For example, Full HD (or 1080p) refers to 1920 × 1080 pixels per video frame. But recording at this definition can lead to extremely large files that are difficult to store and transfer. Thus, evaluators should make sure that their cameras can also record in *lower* definition. For example, 480p (640 × 480 pixels) is usually more than enough for most evaluation projects. The lower density will require much less storage space and will transfer much faster. Obviously, requirements will vary depending on the type of your evaluation and the amount of data you intend to collect, but exorbitantly large file sizes can easily lead to data loss or incomplete data and expensive cloud storage fees.

If you are going to invest money in equipment, the quality of audio is crucially important and difficult to get right, particularly in informal environments. Open and crowded exhibit halls with hard walls and floors, or outdoor spaces full of ambient noise, are especially problematic for capturing reasonably high-quality audio. To make matters worse, digital interactive exhibits tend to generate their own noises (cooling fans, sound effects, music, and voice-over narratives). Picking out dialogue between soft-voiced visitors speaking close to one another can be extremely difficult. The use of relatively inexpensive voice recorders can be a good way to capture visitor speech, especially since recorders can be unobtrusively placed closer to visitors than video cameras. You can even ask visitors to wear small voice recorders on a lanyard.

If that still is not good enough, it might be worthwhile to invest in more serious recording equipment. A detailed guide to audio equipment is beyond the scope of this chapter, but three general rules of thumb apply: First, the cost of equipment roughly corresponds to quality. Second, good audio equipment has a much longer useful lifespan than video equipment, which tends to become obsolete much more quickly. And third, higher quality audio does not necessarily correspond to dramatically larger file sizes. Even a large amount of audio tends to be manageable in terms of digital storage and transfer.

WORKING WITH COMPUTER LOG DATA

One advantage of working with digital exhibits is that it is often possible to augment evaluations with computer-generated log data. In other words, as an exhibit runs, it can record information about what visitors are doing. This information is typically stored as text files in "machine-readable" formats such as comma-separated value or JavaScript Object Notation (JSON).

The granularity of log data ranges from low-level input data (e.g., the time and location of each and every touch point on the screen) to higher level actions that visitors are performing (e.g., the user zoomed in to a picture of a chimpanzee). In some cases, log data can even include screen shots or even small video recordings.

Computer log data can be a treasure trove, but logs can just as easily be overwhelming and sometimes misleading. Some of the most obvious uses of log data involve answering direct questions such as how long did visitors spend interacting with the exhibit, what features were used most or least often, what did visitors do first, and what did they do last before leaving.

But it is also possible to think about harder, less direct questions like what is confusing for visitors, where do they get frustrated, how do people collaborate, and what are different pathways to learning? Oftentimes, these harder questions can be addressed with a combination of log data, video recording, and direct observations. In particular, log data can be a great way to confirm or contradict hunches or hypotheses formed while observing visitor interaction. For example, an evaluator might note that visitors seem more engaged and spend more time if they discover some feature in the first minute of interaction with an exhibit. This kind of hypothesis is easy to confirm quantitatively with log data and adequate technical expertise.

Table 10.1   A short excerpt from an exhibit log file in CSV (Comma Separated Values, standard file) format.

```
TIMESTAMP,EVENT_TYPE,DATA
634777869577061256,LOG_STARTED,July 13 2012 2:35:57 PM
634777869577101256,APP_STARTED,
634777869659781256,FOCAL_NODE_CHANGED,TOLWEB/1
634777869781111256,CONDITION_SELECTED,DT_ONLY
634777869781521256,TOUCH_PROMPT_SHOWN,
634777869862561256,EVALUATION_START,28; Field
634777870078351256,TOP_IMAGE_HOLD_START,TOLWEB/44
634777870079291256,TOP_IMAGE_HOLD_END,TOLWEB/44
634777870135731256,MANUAL_NAV_START,690.14;490.49
634777870145341256,TOP_IMAGE_HOLD_END,TOLWEB/44
634777870148971256,TOP_IMAGE_HOLD_START,TOLWEB/44
634777870158861256,TOP_IMAGE_HOLD_END,TOLWEB/44
634777870158861256,TOP_IMAGE_ZOOMED,TOLWEB/44;2.98
634777870159381256,MANUAL_NAV_END,530.91;494.23
```

Each line records an individual event, and each column contains a data field for that event. For example, the first column shows a "timestamp" with the exact moment at which the event took place as measured by the computer's clock. The second column shows the type of event, while the remaining columns show specific attributes of the event such as the location of a visitor's finger on the screen.

Unfortunately, as should be obvious from looking at Table 10.1, using log data to answer these kinds of questions almost always requires some degree of technical know-how. Logs will have to be extracted and trimmed to times of interest and then synchronized with other data such as field notes, video, or audio streams. Data will then often have to be "cleaned" or transformed in some further way to be useful. For example, it might be important to identify long gaps between timestamps as a likely indicator of a transition from one visitor group to the next. This sort of work is typically done by writing short computer programs using a scripting language like Python. The good news is that user-friendly tools are beginning to emerge for collecting and analyzing log data on various platforms that do not require serious computer programming abilities. For example, Google Analytics is a useful tool for dealing with exhibits built with web technologies, and there are several apps that will record event data on mobile devices like smartphones and tablet computers. These and other tools will continue to improve to support more out-of-the-box solutions for evaluation teams.

EMBEDDED SURVEYS AND QUESTIONNAIRES

An alternative form of automated data collection that directly relates to methods covered in other parts of this book is to build short questionnaires or assessments directly into interactive exhibit. This works especially well for touchscreen interactives that tend to be used by one or two visitors at a time. The idea is to ask very short, unobtrusive questions that check for understanding, engagement, or motivation. Individual items are pulled from a larger bank of questions and then distributed across many visitors. No one person would answer more than one or two questions, but the aggregated responses of many visitors might give insight into effectiveness. For example, you might insert one question near the beginning of a session and another question near the end as a way to gauge shifts in visitor understanding. A similar strategy could be used across multiple elements of larger exhibits. For example, you might ask one question near the entrance to an exhibit hall and a similar question near the exit. Coupling such questions with short demographic surveys (asking about age or the size of visitor groups) might enhance the insight and accuracy of your conclusions. In all cases, the computer prompts visitors and stores their responses for later analysis. This level of automation makes it easy to collect data over long periods of time with minimal human involvement or effort.

In using this method, there is a trade-off between the quality of data collected and its quantity. In other words, with automated approaches, you get *more* data that you can trust *less* than if it were collected by hand. So, as is the case with other methods discussed in this book, it is often most effective when used in conjunction with other tools and methods. To help improve reliability, all questions should be pilot tested first to make sure that visitors understand the prompts and give reasonable responses. It is important that questions work with a diverse cross section of your audience, especially for visitors of different ages and language backgrounds. These are standard guidelines for every survey or questionnaire, but it is also important to observe visitors to make sure that they respond to questions prompted by a computer as they would to questions prompted by a human. It is never safe to assume that visitors will give the same level of attention to (or, for that matter, even read) questions on a computer screen. Finally, be extremely careful not to annoy or frustrate visitors by pestering them with survey questions when they just want to use an exhibit. Keep questions extremely short, to the point, and limited in number. With this in mind, it is best if the questions integrate as naturally as possible into the flow of the experience. With interactive games, for example, it might be possible to blend assessment questions seamlessly into the game experience itself.

To deploy surveys and questionnaires, tools like Qualtrics, File Maker Pro, and Google Forms are easy to use and handle both the front-end presentation and data collection and storage. However, in most cases, custom work of varying complexity will need to be done to seamlessly embed the questions into the larger interactive experience.

SUMMARY

This chapter reviewed some techniques and pitfalls for the evaluation of digital exhibits. The most important takeaway is not to be intimidated by new technology, no matter how expensive or impressive. It is not uncommon for the quality of the visitor experience to be neglected when new or elaborate technology is incorporated into exhibits. The role of the evaluator is to look first and foremost at the human side of the experience. Are people engaged and learning, or are they distracted and confused? Are they talking with one another and exploring together, or do they seem isolated and antisocial?

The other important takeaway is to think about the possibility of automating aspects of your data collection process. When computers are involved in running exhibits, there are opportunities to offload some of the work onto the machines. This can include computer logs, screen capture recordings, or even questionnaire responses. If members of your team have technical expertise, these can be useful additions to your repertoire of evaluation techniques.

Part IV

EVALUATION AS PRACTICE

In the final phase of evaluation, you are usually asked to share your results and conclusions with people who have interest in the study. These might include funding agencies, administrators and staff, members of various community groups, and in many cases, other museum professionals. Ideally, you will offer specific recommendations to help these constituencies act on your results. The process works best when the evaluator has maintained communication with these interested individuals from the outset of the study, getting their input on the study's design, keeping them informed of important decisions, updating them with critical results, and engaging them in discussion about how they will use the results and in what form they would best be shared.

All too often, evaluation reports are stored away with little or no follow-up. In this section, we offer suggestions for making reports more accessible through publication of studies in journals and on the web. We also discuss how to make findings and recommendations more understandable to help translate results into practice.

Chapter 11

Making Evaluation Count

Evaluation reports can be presented in various formats, ranging from a comprehensive description to a brief oral presentation of the findings. The choice depends on the purpose of the study and the needs of the intended users. In many cases, multiple reporting strategies may be required to reach a variety of different interested people. This chapter highlights some of the more common reporting formats and identifies some key principles guiding the presentation of evaluation findings.

REPORTING FORMATS

The most common format for sharing evaluation findings is based on the organization of scientific papers. The advantage of this approach is that it is comprehensive and detailed, providing insight into both the process of the study and its results. A disadvantage is that this approach can be costly and may appear overly technical. A scientifically based format is most useful for summative evaluation, which can be closer in nature to a research study that would have results applicable to other institutions. This report format typically entails the following:

- Abstract
- Introduction
- Methods
- Results
- Conclusions and Summary
- Bibliography

An abstract is a brief description of the entire evaluation project. In one paragraph, state the purpose of the study, a brief description of the methods, the primary results, and the importance of the findings. The abstract should be a brief, but clear, overview of the entire study, so that readers can quickly determine its relevance to their interests. Keep in mind that many people may read only the abstract, so it needs to provide a succinct, compelling summary of the why, who, when, how, and what of the study.

The introduction includes a description of the study's purpose, a brief description or history of the institution or exhibit being studied, and, if relevant, a review of previous work that has some bearing on the purpose, methods, or results. Most importantly, the introduction should clearly state the objectives of the study—the guiding issues or questions that drove it—so that the reader has this context in mind. In addition, the report should provide a sufficient description of the actual phenomenon evaluated (i.e., exhibit, program, or institution). All too often evaluation reports are written as though all readers are as familiar with the phenomenon as are the individuals who commissioned the study. A detailed description of the exhibition or program ensures wider appeal and applicability of the report.

Sometimes the introduction will contain a literature review summarizing previous work or describing studies that used similar methodologies or that influenced the choice of methodology used in your study. Such a summary strengthens the report, adding context and situating the findings within a larger literature base. It shows you are aware of the previous work in your area and that you have made every effort to build on what has already been learned. Not all evaluation budgets can support a literature review, however, so it may not be feasible within your study.

Where a review is included, it should summarize what is already known about the problem or issue you are investigating. For example, if you plan to study the behavior of families in a zoo, you should describe previous studies on this topic. Literature reviews in informal education can sometimes be difficult because the relevant studies are published in many different places. Evaluation studies may be found in journals from the arts and humanities, from education and science education, and from those focused on museums, social science, or general science. In addition, many evaluation reports are not made public. A useful starting point is http://www.informalscience.org, where many summative evaluation reports are posted, including those funded by the National Science Foundation.

The methods section should summarize your data-gathering techniques in detail. Describe who your participants were, how many there were, and how they were sampled. Explain how you collected your data (e.g., if you interviewed your participants, how many questions were asked, how long the interviews lasted, and how you coded the responses). If you conducted observations, include what categories of behaviors you used and how you established them. If you used a questionnaire, include how many questions were asked, where subjects filled it out, and how it was returned. Essentially, the presentation of the methods should be sufficiently detailed to allow another evaluator to replicate your study. Sometimes, it is useful to include a more detailed description of the setting for your study in the methods. For example, if you were collecting tracings of visitors' movements throughout a museum, it could be helpful to provide a map of the galleries with a brief overview of their contents. This helps the reader to visualize the setting for your study and can make the results easier to understand. It can also be useful to include your instruments and protocols as appendices or to post them on the web; this allows others to better interpret your findings and potentially to build on your methods.

The results are where the findings of your study are presented. How the findings are organized may be crucial to their usefulness. Your results may include both qualitative and quantitative information. You may be able to say something about the demographics of visitors because you gathered detailed information on a sample, even if the primary purpose of your study was not to survey the audience. Be sure to examine all aspects of your data and then be strategic about what information would be useful to your readers. Next, consider how the data should be organized. A quality evaluation report should tell a story, one that is keyed to the intended users. Typically, the story revolves around your initial evaluation objectives, since these can serve as a useful framework for organizing your findings. Remember that you do not need to present interview or questionnaire results in the order that the questions were asked. They are ordered in the interview to make them easy for the subjects to understand and to reduce biases. For a report, however, they should be arranged to make them comprehensible to the reader and to emphasize critical findings. Preferably, group the findings into similar headings or themes and present them in order of their relative importance.

It is usually helpful to present quantitative information in graphs or tables so that patterns are easy to recognize. The results section text should describe the major findings and should point out the figures or tables to the reader. Qualitative parts of your study are usually presented in a series of descriptions in the text. When you have much detailed information to present, you may choose to provide a separate section in which to describe each major theme. Graphics, photographs, or diagrams can also be useful in summarizing qualitative or quantitative information.

The conclusions should state what is important about your results. Do not just restate the results, but describe how your findings are relevant to your intended readers. Did your data support the results of previous work in this area? Did it contradict some other work? Did it raise new issues that have not

been discussed before? Informal education evaluation is often quite exploratory, and the results of a study can raise more questions than they answer.
This can be useful for deciding what direction to take in future research.
In the conclusions, examine the big picture: what is happening in your study
site and what the results of your study imply for other similar situations.

Often, an evaluation study is problem centered, and the readers will want
to know what solutions or recommendations you can offer. Staff may want
to know, for example, why so few visitors enter a particular gallery. Your
results may describe where visitors actually go, and how they made decisions
about their movements. In the conclusions, present your best notions, based
on your findings, of why the visitors chose one gallery over another. It is fair
to be speculative, as long as you base your conclusions on the data you have
presented in the report.

The bibliography is the last section. It includes the references that you cite
in your report. If you plan to submit your article for publication, you will
have to tailor the format of your article to the preferred style for the particular
journal where you plan to submit. The *Publication Manual of the American
Psychological Association* (2010) advises on items such as the proper format
for graphs, tables, bibliographies, how to cite references in the text, what to
do with notes, abbreviations, and capitalizations, and how to insure nonsexist
language.

Increasingly, videos, blogs, or photo journals can be effective ways to convey the results of an evaluation study to interested people. Oral debriefings
may be requested in addition to written or multimedia reports. Presentations
made to boards, staff, or community groups can help highlight the most
important study findings and the next steps for improved practice. At the
beginning of the study, make sure you establish the desired format for the
report, so that you can prepare the necessary documentation throughout the
course of your study.

Brief Report

There are times when a brief summary report is most useful, either on its
own or accompanied by a traditional lengthy report. Brief reports can take
many different forms, depending on the purpose of the evaluation study. For
example, formative evaluation tends to be more "quick and dirty" in implementation. It is designed to provide immediate, iterative feedback that will
inform design and decision making, often within a short time frame. As such,
formative reports may be more useful if they are brief in nature, focusing
almost entirely on the results themselves and what those results mean for the
next steps in the project. Unlike a detailed report, which includes sections on
the background of the project and extensive descriptions of the methods, a

brief formative report typically provides only a short abstract of these. The essence of a brief formative report is the findings themselves, presented in bulleted or condensed form.

In a summative evaluation, a brief report may look more like an extended abstract than a scientific report. It provides a succinct summary of the project background and methods and presents highlights from the findings. Generally, extensive tables or long participant quotes are not included; instead, the writer summarizes the major findings and provides only the most relevant data. Further information are put into appendices or included in a longer background report that addresses study details.

In our experience, evaluators sometimes assume that brief reports are easier to write, because their scope is more narrowly defined. However, it is can be more challenging to produce a high-quality brief report that communicates ideas clearly. It sometimes requires that the evaluator first write a detailed manuscript and afterward create a more succinct version that serves as a brief report.

KEY PRINCIPLES FOR REPORTING

Regardless of which reporting format you choose, the following guidelines from Patton (2008) can help you to ensure that your evaluation report is useful:

- *Think about the purpose of the report and its end users.* Ask the staff and other interested people how they plan to use the evaluation findings. To whom do they need to disseminate evaluation results and in what ways? Answers to these questions will influence not only which reporting format you use but also the decisions you make about how to present the findings, and how detailed and technical you are throughout the report.
- *Avoid surprises.* Often, it is helpful to share evaluation findings orally with interested people prior to writing the report. This helps them to better understand the results themselves and to participate in decisions about what is most important to present. Asking staff and others for feedback on an outline of the report can be a useful way of building consensus around reporting strategies and avoiding any surprises.
- *Do not skip the recommendations.* Too often, evaluation reports simply end with conclusions. But unlike research, evaluation is designed to solve problems and to inform practice within a particular context. It is the evaluator's responsibility to suggest what the findings might mean for the institution or program in a practical manner. If the study's purpose was to investigate a program's effectiveness in meeting its goals, the report should not only

decide how effective the program was but also share any insights about how or why it worked or what practices might be changed to improve the program. The evaluator should always be clear about whether recommendations are based on data or on the evaluator's own insights.

- *Dissemination is not the same as use.* Although evaluation reports may be written for specific interested parties, they often have broader applicability for informing others in the field. As such, evaluators are encouraged to publish their studies in recognized journals and to present the findings at conferences. However, writing an evaluation report and publishing evaluation findings are two separate endeavors with distinct goals and approaches. A report is designed to meet the needs of specific interested people, whereas a publication is written for a broader audience of researchers or practitioners in the field and conforms to guidelines laid out for a specific journal.

TRANSLATING EVALUATION FINDINGS INTO PRACTICE

In most instances, evaluations conducted in informal learning environments are intended to inform practice. The evaluator thus serves as a translator to make the findings meaningful for the needs of the project. There is no formula for translating evaluation results into practice, but careful consideration of the purpose of the study and its audience can help make the findings more applicable for practitioners. It is usually best to translate evaluation findings separately for front-end, formative, and summative evaluations, although in practice, these can overlap substantially.

In front-end evaluation, the focus is often on the project's audience and context. Evaluators need to consider the *who* and the *what*: *who* of the project players need *what* kind of information to make a difference? The graphic artist on an exhibit's project may not realize the limitations that potential audience members have for reading fine print. The audio producer may not be aware that youth in a particular target market no longer listen to the radio. The youth activity coordinator may not be familiar with similar activities being conducted in school. In this sense, the evaluator should consider how to target certain kinds of findings to the individuals who will most benefit from the information.

In formative evaluation, a direct line of communication to project developers or decision makers is vital to making study results useful. Sometimes, multiple lines of communication are necessary. For example, during development of the Explore Evolution exhibits funded by the National Science Foundation, a prototype of the entire exhibit gallery was opened to the public at the Science Museum of Minnesota. Evaluators observed and interviewed visitors, and then summarized their findings. The team provided different kinds of communication to different constituents: They met with the museum directors, shared their preliminary findings, and then discussed recommendations for changes. The team then created specific feedback for the exhibit developers to guide them as they made revisions for the final version of the gallery. Additionally, because the copywriter was a science journalist, they prepared additional guidelines to improve text that was not understood well by visitors. Finally, the team published a short report on the project for evolutionary scientists who might want to participate in a similar project (Diamond & Evans 2007). One report may have seemed efficient, but in practice, the different participants required individually tailored feedback.

The timeliness of formative evaluation is also important. Because formative evaluation is intended to assist in the development or design process, it is crucial for the results to be shared quickly in ways that permit their incorporation into the design or construction. For instance, a written report may not be as useful as oral feedback immediately following data collection, where initial trends and patterns are shared within the exhibit developers' timeline.

Summative evaluation can pose the most difficult translation challenge. Typically, summative studies tend to emphasize project outcomes and impacts. Summative studies are useful not only for the project at hand but also for similar future projects. This can mean that different interests are at play when thinking about accessibility and applicability. Having met the funding agencies' requirements, many summative evaluation reports are stored away, never consulted, or considered relevant for future projects. Making a summative evaluation report public can be beyond an evaluator's control. However, under the right circumstances, there are things that can be done to increase access to summative evaluation findings:

- Make the summative evaluation report available to colleagues in the field. For instance, posting the report on www.informalscience.org is a simple way to ensure that both evaluators and practitioners will have access to the results.
- Publish the summative evaluation in the relevant literature. This requires client approval, but it contributes to the field by providing information and examples that other practitioners can build upon.
- Present the summative evaluation at local, regional, or national meetings. Assuming your clients agree, this provides opportunities for discussion about the project that can have far-reaching influence within the field.

There is a gap between research and practice that can prevent evaluation results from being acted on. Evaluators can help bridge that gap by involving interested people at important points in the evaluation process and then

encouraging their participation in debriefing meetings following the completion of the study. This increases the likelihood that others will feel invested
in the study and allows them to better understand the process itself. Evaluators can help interested people better understand the rigor and complexities
of data collection and analysis, as well as the decisions that are made as part
of those processes. In this way the mystery of the evaluation process can be
stripped away. This facilitates reflective conversation about what the results
mean for the institution and helps staff to think concretely about potential
next steps. With a better understanding of how evaluation is done, staff and
other interested people will be better equipped to think about how the results
might apply to their practices.

Regardless of their specific role, evaluators are always partners in a project.
Evaluators work closely with project participants, audience members, and
other interested individuals to help a project realize its goals, sometimes find
new goals, and occasionally realize opportunities that were never imagined
during planning. The translation of evaluation findings into practice often
goes well beyond a particular project. It can be a career-long endeavor that
helps the entire field of informal education improve its practices.

EVALUATION AS IMMERSION

Evaluation is less about data collection than it is about immersion. It is about
becoming so familiar with an institution, exhibit, or program that it becomes
second nature. Whether the data you collect is qualitative, quantitative, or a
combination of both, it will be your intuitive understanding of the opportunities and limitations of the informal culture that will be a primary guide for
your study. Robert Stake cautions that accumulating large data sets is not
enough:

> The key mistake, I think, is the assumption that objective information can be
> aggregated across large numbers of students or visitors to provide a basis for
> decision making to people who are not personally acquainted with the program.
> The key hope, I think, is that subjective information based on key issues, ori-
> ented to real problems and particular situations, rigorously cross-examined,
> will become a standard offering of evaluation studies. (Smithsonian Institution
> 1979, p. 16)

Everyone who has ever worked in a museum, zoo, or botanical garden is
an expert to some degree on how visitors experience their institution. And
yet the findings of an evaluation report may still be surprising. We should
wonder at the depth of some people's experiences, when we expected them to
be superficial. We should consider how quickly some children run through a

museum, when we expected them to stop and look closely. We should remark at how much time some visitors spend at the exhibits, and how briefly others do. And we should marvel when a visitor remembers exactly what sounds the zoo animals made, which dinosaurs were on display, and what flowers were in bloom when they first visited an entire lifetime ago.

References

Ackerman, E. K. 1988. Pathways into a child's mind: Helping children become epistemologists. In *Science learning in the informal setting: Symposium proceedings*, ed. P. G. Heltne and L. A. Marquardt, 7–19. Chicago: Chicago Academy of Sciences.

Acklie, D. S. 2003. *Community based science education for fourth to sixth graders: Influences of a female role model*. PhD diss., University of Nebraska, Lincoln.

ADAGE: Assessment Data Aggregator for Game Environments. 2015. [Digital tool] Retrieved from: http://adageapi.org.

Adams, M., Foutz, S., Luke, J. J., & Stein, J. 2005. *Do art museum programs foster critical thinking in elementary students: Research results from a 3-year study of the Isabella Stewart Gardner Museum's School Partnership Program*. Technical research report. Annapolis, MD: Institute for Learning Innovation.

Allen, S. 2002. Looking for learning in visitor talk: A methodological exploration. In *Learning conversations in museums*, ed. G. Leinhardt, K. Crowley, and K. Knutson, 259–303. Mahwah, NJ: Lawrence Erlbaum.

Alt, M. B., & Griggs, S. 1989. *Evaluating the Mankind Discovering Gallery*. Toronto: Royal Ontario Museum.

American Psychological Association. 2010. *Publication Manual of the American Psychological Association*. 6th ed. Washington, DC: American Psychological Association.

Andrews, K. 1979. Teenagers' attitudes about art museums. *Curator: The Museum Journal* 22(3):224–32.

Ash, D. 2004. How families use questions at dioramas: Ideas for exhibit design. *Curator: The Museum Journal* 47(1):84–100.

Bjork, R. A., & Linn, M. C. 2006. The science of learning and the learning of science: Introducing desirable difficulties. *American Psychological Society Observer* 19(3):1–2.

Block, F., Hammerman, J., Horn, M. S., Phillips, B. C., Evans, E. M., Diamond, J., & Shen, C. 2015. Fluid grouping: Quantifying group engagement around interactive tabletop exhibits in the wild. *ACM Conference on Human Factors in Computing Systems* (CHI' 15), ACM Press, 867–76.

Block, F., Horn, M. S., Phillips, B. C., Diamond, J., Evans, E. M., & Shen, C. 2012. The DeepTree exhibit: Visualizing the tree of life to facilitate informal learning. *IEEE Transactions on Visualization and Computer Graphics* 18(12):2789–98.

Borun, M., Chambers, M., & Cleghorn, A. 1996. Families are learning in science museums. *Curator: The Museum Journal* 39(2):123–38.

Brady, J. 1977. *The craft of interviewing.* New York: Random House.

Carey, S. 1997. Conceptual change. *Journal of Applied Developmental Psychology* 21(1):13–19.

Chipman, G., Druin, A., Beer, D., Fails, J. A., Guha, M. L., & Simms, S. 2006, June. A case study of tangible flags: a collaborative technology to enhance field trips. In *Proceedings of the 2006 conference on interaction design and children* (pp. 1–8). ACM.

Cleveland, W. S. 1985. *The elements of graphing data.* Monterey, CA: Wadsworth Advanced Books and Software.

Crowley, K., Callanan, M. A., Jipson, J., Galco, J., Topping, K., & Shrager, J. 2001. Shared scientific thinking in everyday parent-child activity. *Science Education* 85(6):712–32.

Davis, P., Horn, M., Block, F., Phillips, B., Evans, E. M., Diamond, J., & Shen, C. 2015. "Whoa! We're going deep in the trees!": Patterns of collaboration around an interactive information visualization exhibit. *International Journal of Computer-Supported Collaborative Learning* 10(1):53–76.

Davis, P., Horn, M., & Sherin, B. 2013. The right kind of wrong: A "knowledge in pieces" approach to science learning in museums. *Curator* 56(1):31–46.

Department of Health, Education, and Welfare. 1979. *The Belmont report. Ethical principles and guidelines for the protection of human subjects of research.* Washington, DC: U.S. Government Printing Office.

DeVellis, R. F. 2003. *Scale development: Theory and applications.* 2nd ed. Vol. 26 of *Applied social science research methods.* Thousand Oaks, CA: Sage Publications.

Diamond, J. 1980. The ethology of teaching: A perspective from the observations of families in science museums. PhD diss., University of California, Berkeley.

———. 1982. Ethology in museums: Understanding the learning process. *Round-table Reports* 7(4):13–15.

———. 1986. The behavior of family groups in science museums. *Curator: The Museum Journal* 29(2):139–54.

———. 1991. Prototyping interactive exhibits on rocks and minerals. *Curator: The Museum Journal* 34(1):5–17.

———. 1996. Playing and learning. *ASTC Newsletter* 24(4):2–6.

Diamond, J., & Bond, A. 1999. *Kea, bird of paradox; The evolution and behavior of a New Zealand parrot.* Berkeley: University of California Press.

———. 2013. *Concealing coloration in animals.* Cambridge: Belnap/Harvard University Press.

Diamond, J., & Evans, E. M. 2007. Museums teach evolution. *Evolution* 61:1500–6.

Diamond, J., Evans, E. M., & Spiegel, A. 2012 Walking whales and singing flies: An evolution exhibit and assessment of its impact. In *Evolution challenges: integrating research and practice.* Rosengren, K. R., et. al. (eds.). Oxford: Oxford University Press.

Diamond, J., Hochman, G., Gardner, S., & Schenker, B. 1996. Multimedia science kits: Museum project on the research of women scientists. *Curator* 39:172–87.

Diamond, J., Smith, A., & Bond, A. 1988. California Academy of Sciences Discovery Room. *Curator: The Museum Journal* 31(3):157–66.

Diamond, J., St. John, M., Cleary, B., & Librero, D. 1987. The Exploratorium's Explainer Program: The long-term impacts on teenagers of teaching science to the public. *Science Education* 71(5):643–56.

Diamond, J., Zimmer, C., Evans, E. M., Allison, L., & Disbrow, S. 2005. *Virus and the Whale: Exploring Evolution in Creatures Small and Large.* Arlington, VA: National Science Teachers Association Press.

Dierking, L. D. 1987. Parent-Child interactions in free-choice learning settings: An examination of attention-directing behaviors. *Dissertation Abstracts International* 49(4):778A.

Dierking, L. D., & Pollock, W. 1998. *Questioning assumptions: An introduction to front-end studies in museums.* Washington, DC: Association of Science and Technology Centers.

Dienes, Z., & Berry, D. 1997. Implicit learning: Below the subjective threshold. *Psychonomic Bulletin and Review* (1):3–23.

Dillman, D. A., Smyth, J. D., & Christian, L. M. 2014. *Internet, phone, mail, and mixed-mode surveys: The tailored design method.* 4th ed. New York: John Wiley & Sons.

Ellenbogen, K., Luke, J. J., & Dierking, L. D. 2004. Family learning research in museums: An emerging disciplinary matrix? *Science Education* 88(S1):S48–S58.

Evans, E. M. 2000. The emergence of beliefs about the origins of species in school-age children. *Merrill-Palmer Quarterly* 46(2):221–54.

———. 2005. Teaching and learning about evolution. In *Virus and the whale: Exploring evolution in creatures small and large*, ed., J. Diamond et al., 25–37. Arlington, VA: National Science Teachers Association Press.

Evans, E. M., Spiegel, A., Gram, W., Frazier, B. F., Thompson, S., Tare, M., & Diamond, J. 2009. A conceptual guide to museum visitors' understanding of evolution. *Journal of Science Teaching* 47(3):326–353

Evans, E. M., Spiegel, A., Gram, W., & Diamond, J. 2009. Integrating developmental and free-choice learning frameworks to investigate conceptual change in visitor understanding. VSA Articles, Center for the Advancement of Informal Science Education, *BriefCAISE* January/February, Issue 5, available at http://caise.insci. org/news/62/51/briefCAISE---Jan-Feb-2009-Issue-5.

Falk, J. H. 1983. Time and behavior as predictors of learning. *Science Education* 67(2):267–76.

———, ed. 2001. *Free-choice science education.* New York: Teachers College Press.

———. 2004. The director's cut: Toward an improved understanding of learning from museums. *Science Education* 88(1):S83–S96.

———. 2006. The impact of visit motivation on learning: Using identity as a construct to understand the visitor experience. *Curator: The Museum Journal* 49(2):151–66.

Falk, J. H., & Dierking, L. D. 1992. *The museum experience.* Washington, DC: Whalesback Books.

Falk, J. H. & Holland, D. G. 1991. *Summative evaluation of "Circa 1492: Art in the age of discovery" National Gallery of Art.* Annapolis, MD: Science Learning, Inc.

Fallik, O., Rosenfeld, S., & Eylon, B. 2013. School and out-of-school science: a model for bridging the gap. *Studies in Science Education* 49:69–91.

Feher, E. 1990. Interactive museum exhibits as tools for learning: Explorations with light. *International Journal of Science Education* 12(1):35–49.

Feher, E., & Meyer, K. R. 1992. Children's conceptions of color. *Journal of Research in Science Teaching* 29(5):505–20.

Feher, E., & Rice, K. 1985. Development of scientific concepts through the use of interactive exhibits in a museum. *Curator: The Museum Journal* 28(1):35–46.

Fischer, D. K. 1997. Visitor panels: In-house evaluation of exhibit interpretation. In *Visitor studies: Theory, research and practice.* Vol. 9, ed. M. Willis and R. Loomis, 51–62. Jacksonville, FL: Visitor Studies Association.

Flagg, B. N. 1990. *Formative evaluation for educational technologies.* Hillsdale, NJ: Lawrence Erlbaum Associates.

Foutz, S., & Koke, J. 2007. *Community science learning through youth astronomy apprenticeships: MIT Kavli Institute of Education and Public Outreach—Formative evaluation.* Technical evaluation report. Edgewater, MD: Institute for Learning Innovation.

Friedman, A., ed. 2008. *Framework for evaluating impacts of informal science education projects.* Available at http://informalscience.org/documents/Eval_Framework.pdf.

Frierson, H. T., Hood, S., & Hughes, G. B. 2002. *The 2002 user friendly handbook for project evaluation.* Arlington, VA: National Science Foundation.

Gallistel, C. R. 1990. *The organization of learning.* Cambridge: MIT Press.

Griggs, S. A., & Manning, J. 1983. The predictive validity of formative evaluation of exhibits. *Museum Studies Journal* 1(1):31–41.

Hofstein, A., & Rosenfeld, S. 1996. Bridging the gap between formal and informal science learning. *Studies in Science Education* 28:87–112.

Hood, M. G., & Roberts, L. C. 1994. Neither too young nor too old: A comparison of visitor characteristics. *Curator: The Museum Journal* 37(1):36–45.

Hooper-Greenhill, E. 1994. *Museums and their visitors.* London: Routledge.

Horn, M. S., Crouser, R. J., & Bers, M. U. 2012. Tangible interaction and learning: the case for a hybrid approach. *Personal and Ubiquitous Computing* 16(4):379–89.

Jee, B., Uttal, D., Spiegel, A., & Diamond, J. 2015. Expert-novice differences in mental models of viruses, vaccines, and the causes of infectious disease. *Public Understanding of Science* 24(2):241–56.

Jolly, E. J. 2002. On the quest for cultural context in evaluation: Non ceteris paribus. Paper presented at a National Science Foundation Directorate for Education and Human Resources workshop, Arlington, VA, April 25–26, 2002.

Klein, M. 1981. Recall versus recognition. In *Activities handbook for the teaching of psychology,* ed. L. T. Benjamin Jr. and K. D. Lowman, 79–80. Washington, DC: American Psychological Association.

Koepfler, J. A., Heimlich, J. E., & Yocco, V. S. 2010. Communicating Climate Change to Visitors of Informal Science Environments. *Applied Environmental Education and Communication* 9(4):233–42.

Korn, R. 1995. An analysis of differences between visitors at natural history museums and science centers. *Curator: The Museum Journal* 38(3):150–60.

Kosslyn, S. M. 2006. *Graph design for the eye and mind.* Oxford: Oxford University Press.

Kosslyn, S. M., Heldmeyer, K. H., & Locklear, E. P. 1980. Children's drawings as data about their internal representations. *Journal of Experimental Child Psychology* 23:191–211.

Kubota, C. A., & Olstad, R. G. 1991. Effects of novelty-reducing preparation on exploratory behavior and cognitive learning in a science museum setting. *Journal of Research in Science Teaching* 28(3):225–34.

Larkin, J. 1989. Display-based problem solving. In *21st century Carnegie-Mellon symposium on cognition, complex information processing: The impact of Herbert A. Simon*, ed. Klahr, D., & Kotovsky, K., 319–41. Hillsdale, NJ: Lawrence Erlbaum.

Larkin, J., & Rainard. B. 1984. A research methodology for studying how people think. *Journal of Research in Science Teaching* 21(3):235–54.

Lazlo, E., Artigiani, R., Combs, A., & Csányi, V. 1996. *Changing visions, human cognitive maps: Past, present, and future.* Westport, CO: Praeger.

Lee, S. A., Bumbacher, E., Chung, A. M., Cira, N., Walker, B., Park, J. Y., . . . & Riedel-Kruse, I. H. 2015, April. Trap it!: A Playful Human-Biology Interaction for a Museum Installation. In *Proceedings of the 33rd Annual ACM Conference on Human Factors in Computing Systems* (pp. 2593–602). ACM.

Leinhardt, G., Crowley, K., & Knutson, K. eds. 2002. *Learning conversations in museums.* Mahwah, NJ: Lawrence Erlbaum.

Loftus, E. F., Levidow, B., & Duensing, S. 1992. Who remembers best? Individual differences in memory for events that occurred in a science museum. *Applied Cognitive Psychology* 6:93–107.

Lorenz, K. Z. 1950. The comparative method in studying innate behavior patterns. *Symposia of the Society for Experimental Biology* 4:221–68.

Louw, M., & Crowley, K. 2013. New ways of looking and learning in natural history museums: The use of gigapixel imaging to bring science and publics together. *Curator: The Museum Journal* 56(1):87–104.

Lucas, A. M., & McManus, P. 1986. Investigating learning from informal sources: Listening to conversations and observing play in science museums. *European Journal of Science Education* 8(4):342–52.

Luke, J. J., Stein, J., Kessler, C., & Dierking, L. D. 2007. Making a difference in the lives of youth: Mapping success with the "Six Cs." *Curator: The Museum Journal* 50(4):417–34.

Luke, J. J., Wadman, M. E., Dierking, L. D., Jones, M. C., & Falk, J. H. 2002. *Summative evaluation of the BoneZone exhibition at The Children's Museum of Indianapolis.* Technical research report. Annapolis, MD: Institute for Learning Innovation.

Lyons, L., Tissenbaum, M., Berland, M., Eydt, R., Wielgus, L., & Mechtley, A. 2015, June. Designing visible engineering: supporting tinkering performances in museums. In *Proceedings of the 14th International Conference on Interaction Design and Children* (pp. 49–58). ACM.

Ma, J., Liao, I., Ma, K. L., & Frazier, J. 2012. Living liquid: Design and evaluation of an exploratory visualization tool for museum visitors. *IEEE Transactions on Visualization and Computer Graphics* 18(12):2799–808.

Ma, J., Sindorf, L., Liao, I., & Frazier, J. 2015, January. Using a Tangible Versus a Multi-touch Graphical User Interface to Support Data Exploration at a Museum Exhibit. In *Proceedings of the Ninth International Conference on Tangible, Embedded, and Embodied Interaction* (pp. 33–40). ACM.

Martin, P., & Bateson, P. 2007. *Measuring behavior: An introductory guide.* 3rd ed. Cambridge: Cambridge University Press.

McLean, K. 1993. *Planning for people in museum exhibitions.* Washington, DC: Association of Science and Technology Centers.

McManus, P. M. 1987. It's the company you keep . . . The social determination of learning-related behaviour in a science museum. *The International Journal of Museum Management and Curatorship* 6:263–70.

———. 1993. Memories as indicators of the impact of museum visits. *Museum Management and Curatorship* 12:367–80.

———. 1989a. Oh yes, they do: How museum visitors read labels and interact with exhibit texts. *Curator: The Museum Journal* 32(3):174–89.

———. 1989b. What research says about learning in science museums: Watch your language! People do read labels. *ASTC Newsletter* 17(3):5–6.

Melton, A. W. 1933. *Problems of installation in museums of art.* Washington, DC: American Association of Museums.

———. 1935. Studies of installation at the Pennsylvania Museum of Art. *Museum News* 12:5–8.

Miles, R. S., Alt, M. B., Gosling, D. C., Lewis, B. N., & Tout. A. F. 1988. *The design of educational exhibits.* London: Unwin Hyman.

Miles, M. B., Huberman, A. M., & Saldaña. 2013. *Qualitative data analysis: A methods sourcebook.* 3rd ed. Thousand Oaks, CA: Sage Publications.

Museum Management Consultants, Inc., & Polaris Research and Development. 1994. *Bay Area Research Project: A multicultural audience study for Bay Area museums.* 2 vols. San Francisco: Bay Area Research Project Consortium.

National Research Council. 2009. *Learning science in informal environments: People, places, and pursuits.* Committee on Learning Science in Informal Environments, ed. P. Bell, B. Lewenstein, A. W. Shouse, & M. A. Feder, Division of Behavioral and Social Sciences and Education. Washington, DC: The National Academies Press.

National Science Foundation. 2000. *The cultural context of educational evaluation: The role of minority evaluation professionals.* Arlington, VA: National Science Foundation.

———. 2002. *The cultural context of educational evaluation: A Native American perspective.* Arlington, VA: National Science Foundation.

———. 2010. *The 2010 User-Friendly Handbook for Project Evaluation.* Arlington, VA: National Science Foundation.

Novak, J. 1977. *A theory of education.* Ithaca: Cornell University Press.

Oppenheimer, F. 1972. The Exploratorium: A playful museum combines perception and art in science education. *American Journal of Physics* 40:978–84.

———. 1980. Adult play. *The Exploratorium Magazine* 3(6):1–3.

———. 1986. *Working prototypes*. San Francisco: The Exploratorium.

Oppenheimer, F., & Cole, K. C. 1974. The Exploratorium: A participatory museum. *Prospects* 4(1):1–10.

Paris, S. G., ed. 2002. *Perspectives on object-centered learning in museums*. Mahwah, NJ: Lawrence Erlbaum Associates.

Patton, M. Q. 1987. *How to use qualitative methods in evaluation.* Newbury Park, CA: Sage Publications, Inc.

———. 1990. *Qualitative evaluation and research methods*. 2nd ed. Newbury Park, CA: Sage Publications, Inc.

———. 2008. *Utilization-focused Evaluation*. 4th ed. Thousand Oaks, CA: Sage Publications, Inc.

Piaget, J. 1973. *To understand is to invent: The future of education*. New York: Penguin Books.

Piaget, J., & Inhelder, B. 1969. *The psychology of the child*. New York: Basic Books.

Pick, H. L., Jr. 1993. Organization of spatial knowledge in children. In *Spatial representation*, ed. N. Eilan, R. McCarthy, and B. Brewer, 31–42. Oxford: Blackwell.

Reif, F., & Larkin, J. H. 1991. Cognition in scientific and everyday domains: Comparison and learning implications. *Journal of Research in Science Teaching* 28(9):733–60.

Roberts, J., Lyons, L., Cafaro, F., & Eydt, R. 2014, June. Interpreting data from within: supporting human-data interaction in museum exhibits through perspective taking. In *Proceedings of the 2014 conference on interaction design and children* (pp. 7–16). ACM.

Robinson, E. S. 1931. Exit the typical museum visitor. *Journal of Adult Education* 3(4):418–23.

Robinson, E. S., Sherman, I. C., & Curry, L. E. 1928. *The behaviour of museum visitors. New Series* 5. Washington, DC: American Association of Museums.

Roediger, H. L. 1990. Implicit memory: Retention without remembering. *American Psychologist* 45(9):1043–56.

Roschelle, J. 1995. Learning in interactive environments: Prior knowledge and new experience. In *Public institutions for personal learning,* ed. J. H. Falk and L. D. Dierking, 37–51. Washington, DC: American Association of Museums.

Rosenfeld, S. 1982. A naturalistic study of visitors at an interactive mini-zoo. *Curator: The Museum Journal* 25(3):187–212.

Salant, P., & Dillman, D. A. 1994. *How to conduct your own survey*. New York: John Wiley & Sons, Inc.

Semper, R. J. 1990. Science museums as environments for learning. *Physics Today* 43(11):50–56.

SenGupta, S., Hopson, R., & Thompson-Robinson, M. 2004. Cultural competence in evaluation: An overview. In *In search of cultural competence in evaluation: Toward principles and practices*. Vol. 102 of *New Directions for Evaluation*, ed. M. Thompson-Robinson, R. Hopson, & S. SenGupta, 5–18. San Francisco: Jossey-Bass.

Serrell, B. 1977. Survey of visitor attitude and awareness at an aquarium. *Curator: The Museum Journal* 20(1):48–52.

———. 1997. Paying attention: The duration and allocation of visitors' time in museum exhibitions. *Curator: The Museum Journal* 40(2):108–25.

Simon, N. 2010. *The participatory museum.* Santa Cruz, California: Museum 2.0.

Singer, D. G., & Golinkoff, R. M. 2006. *Play = learning: How play motivates and enhances children's cognitive and social emotional growth.* Oxford: Oxford University Press.

Smithsonian Institution. 1979. *An abstract of the proceedings of the Museum Evaluation Conference, June 23–24, 1977.* Washington, DC: Smithsonian Institution Office of Museum Programs.

Snibbe, S. S., & Raffle, H. S. 2009, April. Social immersive media: pursuing best practices for multi-user interactive camera/projector exhibits. In *Proceedings of the SIGCHI Conference on Human Factors in Computing Systems* (pp. 1447–56). ACM.

Spiegel, A. N., Evans, E. M., Frazier, B., Hazel, A., Tare, M., Gram, W., & Diamond, J. 2012. Changing museum visitors' conceptions of evolution. *Evolution Education & Outreach* 5:43–61.

Spiegel, A. N., McQuillan, J., Halpin, P., Matuk, C., & Diamond, J. 2013. Engaging teenagers with science through comics. *Research in Science Education* 43(6): 2309–26.

Spiegel, A. N., Rockwell, S. K., Acklie, D. S., Frerichs, S. W., French, K., & Diamond, J. 2005. Wonderwise 4-H: Following in the footsteps of women scientists. *Journal of Extension* [On-line] 43(4), Article 4FEA3.

Spock, M. 1988. What's going on here: Exploring some of the more elusive, subtle signs of science learning. In *Science learning in the informal setting: Symposium proceedings*, ed. P. G. Heltne and L. A. Marquardt, 254–61. Chicago: The Chicago Academy of Sciences.

Storksdieck, M., & Falk, J. H., 2005. Using the contextual model of learning to understand visitor learning from a science center exhibition. *Science Education* 89(5):744–78.

Sudman, S., Bradburn, N., & Schwartz, N. 1996. *Thinking about answers: The application of cognitive processes to survey methodology.* San Francisco: Jossey-Bass.

Tare, M., French, J., Frazier, B. N., Diamond, J., & Evans, E. M. 2011. The importance of explanation: Parents' scaffold children's learning at an evolution exhibition. *Science Education* 95:720–744.

Taylor, S., ed. 1991. *Try it! Improving exhibits through formative evaluation.* Washington, DC: Association of Science-Technology Centers.

Tourangeau, R., Rips, L. J., & Rasinski, K. 2000. *The psychology of survey response.* New York: Cambridge University Press.

Tufte, E. R. 1983. *The visual display of quantitative information.* Cheshire, CT: Graphics Press.

———. 1997. *Visual explanations.* Cheshire, CT: Graphics Press.

Tulving, E., & Schacter, D. L. 1990. Priming and human memory systems. *Science* 247(4940):301–306.

Tukey, J. W. 1977. *EDA: Exploratory data analysis.* Readings, MA: Addison-Wesley.

University of Nebraska-Lincoln Institutional Review Board. 2015. *University of Nebraska-Lincoln Human Research Protections Policies and Procedures.* Lincoln: University of Nebraska.

W. K. Kellogg Foundation. 2004. Logic model development guide. Available at http://www.smartgivers.org/uploads/logicmodelguidepdf.pdf.

Yalowitz, S., & Tomulonis, J. 2004. Jellies: Living art. Summative evaluation.

Yoder, P., & Symons, F. 2010. *Observational measurement of behavior.* New York: Springer Publishing Co.

Yoon, S., Elinich, K., Wang, J., Steinmeier, C., & Tucker, S. 2012. Using augmented reality and knowledge-building scaffolds to improve learning in a science museum. *International Journal of Computer-Supported Collaborative Learning* 7(4):519–41. doi:10.1007/s11412012–9156-x.

Zimmerman, H. T., Reeve, S., & Bell, P. 2010. Family sense-making practices in science center conversations. *Science Education* 94(3):478–505.

Index

Page references for figures are italicized

qualitative:
 methods, 66, 67, 74, 85, 94–98;
 questions, 77, 79;
 sampling, 50–51.
 See also interviews; participant
  observation
quantitative:
 methods, 74, 85, 86–94;
 questions, 66, 76–79;
 sampling, 46–50.
 See also counting visitors; data
  analysis; graphs; interviews;
  observation; tables
quasi-experimental, 5, 6
questionnaire, 75–84;
 examples, *80, 81–83;*
 web, 84.
 See also conceptual change;
  demographic survey; qualitative;
  quantitative
quotations, 43, 60, 96–98

rating scale, 59–60, 70, 78.
 See also interviews; questionnaire
reading, 17, 51, 78, 116;
 labels, 18–19, 19, 44, 57, *60*, 62,
  102.
 See also label text
reasoning patterns. *See* evolution
  reasoning
recall. *See* memory, recall
recognition. *See* memory, recognition
relationship maps. *See* personal meaning
  mapping
reliability, 44, 72, 115
Robinson, Edward, 54, 61, 105

sample size, 44, 45–48, 94
sampling:
 error, 46–47, *46*, 93;
 methods, 50–51, 63–64;
 representative, *48*, 59;
 systematic, 47, 48, *47–48*.
 See also behavioral sampling;
  informants; qualitative, sampling;
  quantitative, sampling

scale. *See* rating scale
school groups, 5, 13, 49
screen capture. *See* video,
  screen capture
self-report measures, 17–18
smartphones, 17, 54, 99, 114
social behavior. *See* behavior, social
social media, xi, 5, 17, 105
statistics. *See* data analysis
subjects. *See* human subjects
summative evaluation, 119, 120, 122,
  124–25
survey, 1, 3, 17, 43, 45, 65, 75–79, *80,
  81–83*, 101, 115–16, 12.
 See also questionnaire

tables, 85, 86, 88–91, *89, 90*, 121–22
tablet computers, 106
tabletop displays, 104
tangible interfaces, 104
task analysis, 22–23, 27–29
teaching, xii, 14, 61
text. *See* label text
thinking. *See* clinical interview;
  cognitive; evolution reasoning;
  interviews; task analysis;
  understanding exhibit
  phenomena
timing. *See* observation, tracking
Tolman, Edward, 29
touchscreens, 102
tracking visitor movements, 44, 53,
  54–56, *55*, 57, 105;
  technology, 105
tree of life exhibit. *See* Life on Earth

ubiquitous computing, 101–5
understanding exhibit phenomena, 4,
  13, 14, 15, 22, 23–24, *24*, 25, 29,
  30, 43.
 See also learning
University of Nebraska State Museum,
  31, 37, *39, 40*

validity, 44
verification, 94, 98

About the Authors

Judy Diamond is professor and curator of informal science education at the University of Nebraska State Museum. As a biologist and science educator, she is the author of over 40 publications on informal learning. She has a long career working in science museums, first as curriculum developer at the Lawrence Hall of Science, as evaluator and project coordinator at the Exploratorium, and as deputy director for public programs at the San Diego Natural History Museum. She earned her doctorate from the SESAME Group at the University of California at Berkeley. She is the senior author of several books, including *Kea, Bird of Paradox: The Evolution and Behavior of a New Zealand Parrot* (1999), *Virus and the Whale: Exploring Evolution in Creatures Small and Large* (2006), and *Concealing Coloration in Animals* (2013).

Michael Horn is assistant professor of learning sciences and computer science at Northwestern University, where he directs the Tangible Interaction Design and Learning Lab. Horn earned a PhD in human-computer interaction from Tufts University in 2009 and has been developing innovative technology-based learning experiences for museum and other informal learning environments for over ten years. His research interests involve understanding the role of cultural forms in shaping participating and learning around physical and technological artifacts. He is the author of over thirty scholarly articles, and his work can be seen at the Museum of Science, Boston, the California Academy of Sciences, the Field Museum, and the Computer History Museum. He recently received a CAREER award from the National Science Foundation to study computational literacy in informal learning environments.

David Uttal is professor of psychology and education at Northwestern University. He holds a doctorate in developmental psychology from the University of Michigan, and he is the author of over seventy-five articles and book chapters. His research interests are in the development of children's thinking, with a focus on symbolic and spatial reasoning, and his work has been supported by the National Institutes of Health, the National Science Foundation, and the Institute of Education Sciences. At Northwestern University, he directed the Multidisciplinary Program in Education Sciences, which trains graduate students from different disciplines to conduct rigorous research in educational contexts. He is also president-elect of the Cognitive Development Society. His research on the malleability of spatial thinking received the 2015 George Miller Award from the American Psychological Association for outstanding contributions to general psychology.